Real Life – Real Laughs

Humor When You Need It Most

Cate Burns

Text Copyright © 2025 by Kaethe Kauffman, Ph.D.

All rights reserved. No part of this book may be used or reproduced in any manner whatsoever without written permission from the publisher, except by a reviewer who may quote brief passages in a review.

Cover illustration: Kaethe Kauffman, "Happy Office Face," collage & oil paint, 10"x8", 2021.
Cover design: Lucy Arnold

ISBN 978-1-950251-16-2 (paperback)
ISBN 978-1-950251-17-9 (eBook)

Library of Congress Control Number: 2025903768
First edition
Printed in the United States of America

Published by The National League of American Pen Women, Inc.

PEN WOMEN PRESS

Founded in 1897, the National League of American Pen Women, Inc. is a nonprofit dedicated to promoting the arts. NLAPW, Inc. 1300 17th Street NW, Washington, D.C. 20036-1973; www.nlapw.org.

Advance Praise for
Real Life—Real Laughs: *Humor When You Need It Most*

"I'm so excited about this new important work. Cate has found a unique, authentic voice, and I want to hear more."

Lynn Andrews, Author

"Absolutely LOVE the descriptions. The connection to chakras, along with the metaphorical richness, is wonderful. Very, very, very clever and, dare I say it? – unique. This is refreshing, funny, inventive, and delightful."

Sharon Whitehill, Ph.D., Editor

"Burns has such mature insights into life. Her wisdom and knowledge awe me. Her honesty is amazing. The book reflects many years of endeavor, searching for her truth."

Pattie Crockett, Book Reviewer

"As Burns writes, holding her pen like a paintbrush, she allows her spectacles to slip down her nose, pauses, reflects, and resumes her work. She is compact in her stillness, her head tilted. She would appear never to have known a moment that was not entirely graced."

Jacqueline Mitchard, Author

"Burns has a gift for imbuing everything she touches or composes with uncanny predetermined significance. She has the remarkable capacity of creating imagery that lingers in the mind long after the reader has turned away. This persistent eidetic imagery sustains itself within the thresholds separating the consciousness and the unconsciousness."

Dominique Nahas, Critic, New York City

"[T]he woman is no longer supplemental to the narrative but, by aggressively taking charge, becomes a forceful participant in the production of meanings."

Irina Costache, Ph. D., Critic. Los Angeles

Dedication

*I dedicate this book to my father,
Richard G. Kauffman, 1916-1957.*

Acknowledgements

Thank you to Carol Egon and Fran Lyons, my writers' critique group, for your astounding and steadfast wisdom year after year, making me more than I could have imagined.

During the pandemic, Kauffman challenged herself to make portraits using only office supplies.

The names and other identifying characteristics of the persons included in this collection of stories have been changed.

Contents

Real Life – Real Laughs

Part One *Through the Needle's Eye* 1
Chapter 1 Augusta Treverorum 2
Chapter 2 To Kill or Not to Kill 6
Chapter 3 Funny Old Soul 11
Chapter 4 People Watching 17
Chapter 5 Mom's Presence 22
Chapter 6 In the Toilet 25
Chapter 7 Conglomerate Catastrophe 30
Chapter 8 Giant Jiminy and Mr. Clean 38
Chapter 9 Zero Testosterone 45
Chapter 10 I am More Mature Than That 50
Part Two *Friends?* 57
Chapter 11 The Seal Who Loved My Sister 58
Chapter 12 Henry IV 63
Chapter 13 Peculiar Confidences 72
Chapter 14 Ultra U 77
Chapter 15 The Older Woman 86
Chapter 16 Smart Water 91
Chapter 17 I Thought I was Interesting 94
Chapter 18 A Good Boy 98
Chapter 19 Busy Birds 100
Part Three *Keeping Sane, Mostly* 103
Chapter 20 Odd Hairdressers 104
Chapter 21 Pandemic Itch 108
Chapter 22 Introvert heaven 112
Chapter 23 Pleased Protoplasm 116
Chapter 24 Kelvins are Forever 120
Chapter 25 Zooming Ever Lower 127

Chapter 26 Red Bed 134
Chapter 27 In the Dark 138
Chapter 28 Crazy 142
Part Four *Being Brave—Or Not* 145
Chapter 29 Cliff Jumping 146
Chapter 30 Paint Boxer 151
Chapter 31 Age Glorious and Victorious 158
Chapter 32 Halo Meditation with Clouds 164
Chapter 33 A Dentist's Secret 169
Chapter 34 Birds of a Feather 173
Chapter 35 Hooked 176
Chapter 36 Being Brave—Or Not 181
Chapter 37 The Last Laugh 185
Chapter 38 Shaman Joy 191

Real Life – Real Laughs

Humor When You Need It Most

Part One

Through the Needle's Eye

James Haydn Kauffman Hite, **Kaethe Kauffman and James Haydn Kauffman Hite, Trier, Germany,** *photo, 2014*

Chapter 1
Augusta Treverorum

As our train slid into the western German city of Trier, large banners festooned the station: *Augusta Treverorum*. My son went nuts. With glistening dark eyes, curly hair and a broad smile, Jon, in his mid-twenties, loudly blurted, "Mom, it's Augusta Treverorum," as if I knew what that meant. "We're here on the spot. I hadn't realized. This is so cool." He twirled, arms wide, in all directions, as if trying to see everything at once while his legs did little jitterbug kicks.

I remained oblivious. As his excitement grew, he seemed to think we had arrived in the promised land, and I could only stare, gape-mouthed, at my normally quiet and reasonable son. I wondered if an incipient schizophrenic personality had emerged, as it sadly did in some young people.

For Jon's entire life, I had promised him a tour to the towns where our distant relatives had lived in Europe. Last summer, he announced he had a free week in September, and it would be perfect for the ancestor trip.

My first thought was, *But we might do that someday in the distant future.* I felt like an old fogey habitually resistant to change, which I'd sworn I would never be. Checking my calendar, I had that week free and I mentally shrugged: the future had arrived.

We knew Trier had Roman ruins and Jon loved Roman military history. But my reserved son was nearly break-dancing with excitement.

"What's it mean, Augusta Treverorum?" I asked, hoping for a non-schizoid answer.

"It's my computer game, you know, the one I play all the time, my favorite."

I groaned but tried to stifle it. We had fought the video game wars during Jon's teen years, due to my certainty that it rotted his gray matter. Since he began college, Jon lived apart from me, and I tried to convince myself that his screen-time was no longer my concern.

"The Roman troops conquered the Celtic people, the Treveri, right here." His cheeks became rosy with his broad gestures and tapping feet.

It felt odd for me to enjoy Jon's big-eyed enthusiasm for a computer game that he'd apparently absorbed at the cellular level. And stranger still, this game had a practical application in the real world, helping us comprehend our family history. A clever German bureaucrat must have known of the game's popularity and made the banners to attract young people.

I shared what little I knew of our Trier ancestors with Jon as we traveled. My great-grandmother, Susanna, had been an orphan in the 1800s and we had one photo of her somber square face with our fair-haired Belgian great-grandfather, Leonard. Susanna must have bequeathed her curly black hair, deep brown eyes and skin several shades duskier than a Celt, to her grandson, my father, and then to me and my son. Genetically, she seemed to be a Celtic-Treveri/Roman fusion, which made sense.

After twenty years of army service, the Roman troops were provided with a generous pension and free land in and around Trier. They tended to remain on conquered land and marry locals, ideally adding a cultural take-over to the military one.

Over five hundred years of Celtic blending with Romans resulted in Susanna. After 475 AD, the Gauls (France and West Germany) and then the Franks (the rest of Germany) alternated in ruling the territory.

But those old Roman warrior genes in our curly black hair, dark eyes and olive skin, persevered to the present day.

As we disembarked from the train, my son, twitching with glee, repeated, "This is it. This is where it all happened," while he searchingly peered around, as if expecting a Roman Centurion to emerge from a corner. "Augustus conquered the Treveri people right where I'm standing." He sighed and I sensed heavy satisfaction. After all, he had fought those wars himself for years, albeit on a computer monitor. Now screen fantasy encountered solid reality.

A new expression came over his face, a look of wonder, "But," he said, "this is where I came from. I'm one of the Treveri. Wait, I'm Roman, too." He stopped, stunned, as he seemed to ponder our hybrid ancestors.

"Oh, my god, this isn't just a game I played," he said. "I'm the result of that war." He gulped, "I **am** the game."

"Wow," I said, loving Jon's insight, "Yes, you are. Or rather, we are."

Then I chuckled, "And it's a miracle I've found a computer game I can finally relate to."

He laughed, "Yeah, Mom, literally."

Chapter 2
To Kill or Not to Kill

Should I kill the spider inching across my table? I sat in a dilemma. I hated insects in my home. And it would be easy to swat it, an instant solution. But as I looked at the little fellow, I remembered Rosie, a tarantula ambassador at a nature exhibit outside Denver, Colorado. With rose-tinted beige furry legs and body, Rosie glowed, the cuddliest spider imaginable, and I wanted to hold her. Rosie seemed relaxed with the handler, Stephanie. But when Stephanie tilted her arm toward mine in a signal for Rosie to walk onto my hand, the spider backed up instead, hesitant. As an introvert, I empathized. I am also reluctant to step toward strangers. My meditation teachers, two Tibetan monks, regularly taught me to have sympathy for all creatures. This has helped me overcome shyness with humans and wildlife, some of whom seemed interchangeable at times.

After a few more arm tilts and encouraging words from Stephanie, Rosie slowly complied, and I felt her tender fuzzy feet on the back of my hand. Thrilled, I savored Rosie's eight tiny footsteps repeatedly tapping like feathers on my skin.

Real Life—Real Laughs

I murmured, "Hi, Rosie. You're so soft and beautiful. Thank you for visiting me."

Rosie performed her diplomat job like a professional, going a few inches up my forearm, giving me a fine tarantula visit. When my time was up, I tilted my arm in Stephanie's direction. At this prompt, Rosie quickly scampered toward her friend, seemingly overjoyed. The insect's body language appeared so clear, I felt compassion well up in me, just as the Tibetan lamas had suggested could eventually happen. But I never dreamed I would sympathize with a giant, hairy spider.

Since my visit with Rosie, who was a perfect emissary for her kind, I could no longer kill her kin. I slid cardboard underneath the spider on my table until it crawled on. Then I gently carried it outdoors.

When I found a cricket living under my couch, I thought of the old-fashioned cartoon character I had loved as a child, cheerful Jiminy Cricket, who instructed us to follow our conscience.

I loved Jiminy and took his lessons to heart, so much so that when I found out a boyfriend had deliberately lied to me for years, philandering when he repeatedly promised me monogamy, I blurted, "But don't you remember Jiminy Cricket?" He didn't.

I found a large drinking glass to place on top of the Jiminy in my living room. But that proved optimistic. A

Real Life—Real Laughs

speedy guy, he hopped away from the glass every time I tried to cover him. I jumped with him around my living room, like his cricket sister doing a crazy dance. After about 15 tries, I succeeded. A little oblong face with big eyes peered up at me, seeming apprehensive, just as I would be if trapped under a glass cage. That I would want to extend goodwill to a leaping insect seemed marvelous. The monks had taught me to attempt it, but I hadn't believed I would ever want to. Now I truly wanted the best for Jiminy, but not under my couch.

I crooned to him, "Jiminy, you are the cutest cricket on Earth, but it's time to live outside."

I read about a prisoner who was so lonely, he made friends with a fly he named Fred. He saved crumbs of food to feed Fred, who became tame and allowed his head and sides to be stroked. Visiting my adult son Jon, one lazy afternoon, we sat outside, and a fly landed on his knee. Naturally, Jon smacked it. My body jolted in shock, and I almost called out, "But that fly could have been your friend."

Although my Buddhist instructors taught that all living beings have been my family members in countless other lifetimes, I remained skeptical on that point. But how could I account for my body's shudder when the fly got hurt, possibly killed? Perhaps I had begun to think of the fly as a fellow being and a potential friend.

Real Life—Real Laughs

While sitting with Jon, I pondered this. I realized fly friendship would not be considered a social norm and I tried to be normal around my son. At age 70, I had a dawning awareness of the possibility that an adult child might seriously suggest assisted living. I had seen it happen to my friends. But I felt badly about the fly, and shouldn't a mother share her deepest beliefs with her child, if the ideas weren't too crazy? Subtly, or so I thought, an hour later, I casually told him the story about the prisoner and Fred. He didn't seem surprised. After all, a few years ago, I had taken him to meet the current incarnation of the Buddha of Compassion, the Dalai Lama.

To be fair to Jon, when I was in my mid-twenties, his age, I didn't save insects. I grew up squashing them like everyone else. Perhaps my meditation trainers had gained modest success after years of coaching me to be kind to all beings, even creepy, crawly ones. Insects and ex-boyfriends seemed to be my litmus test for true compassion.

Bit by bit, I have gained kindheartedness for what I formerly considered disgusting life forms. I'm not sure how or when it happened, but for the last 20 years, my spiritual guides taught me that all sentient life stood united by our experiences of suffering and wanting happiness. Seeing Rosie cringe or Jiminy wary aroused my sympathy.

And I could imagine getting friendly with a fly if I were stuck in solitary confinement.

The lamas helped me find a prayer I could sincerely say for ex-boyfriends, no matter how badly we had ended things. It's called the *Metta Prayer*.

May [his name] and all beings have happiness and the causes of happiness.

May we be free from suffering and the causes of suffering.

May we never be apart from the sacred happiness which is free from suffering.

May we dwell in the great equanimity, impartial, free from attachment and aversion.

Every day, I chanted the last line with enthusiasm because I really wanted Joe, Bill, or Charlie to stop being angry. Slowly, my lingering resentment eased and they stopped harassing me. The prayer worked. Several years after a break-up, I could truly wish the fellow well.

The lamas esteemed ants and refused to kill them. When termites munched the meditation center's wooden structure, even though it broke the lamas' hearts, the destructive bugs had to be exterminated. The monks chanted prayers for those thousands of sentient beings for months. I thought I had done okay on the compassion meter with spiders, crickets, flies, and boyfriends, but I've yet to warm up to ants and termites. More meditation for me.

Chapter 3
Funny Old Soul

James Haydn Kauffman Hite, **A Wild Burro Visits**, *photo, 2024*

    Spiritual growth can be comical. Even when we're laughing at the absurdity of some situations, qualities such as acceptance, gratitude, transformation, grace, meditation, and self-reflection can lead us towards serenity. While not without its difficulties, nevertheless, my son Jon's trajectory through life has been one of the best and funniest soul journeys ever.

At about two years old, soon after Jon learned to talk and sing our favorite songs, I pulled him in a little red wagon around our small community, one of his favorite activities. As he rolled along, all at once, he burst out singing a tune I'd never heard before, "I'm so happy to be alive." He belted the same refrain over and over at decibels that were likely illegal in our quiet forested area. He sang so loudly, our neighbors emerged at every house we approached. When they beheld the toddler in his red wagon singing his heart out, every person laughed, waved, and lingered with wide smiles while we passed.

I felt astounded at Jon's new and unfamiliar tune, and I sported a huge grin on my face like everyone else. All of us seemed to exult in Jon's contagious joy in simply being alive, our gratitude giving us a great lift to our spirits.

At age four, one night before bed, I washed Jon's face and applied rubbing alcohol with a cotton swab to an oily spot around his nose. Suddenly, Jon yelped, "Ouch! That hurts."

I quickly apologized and explained there must be a small scratch I hadn't seen. Oddly, Jon seemed lost in thought. "You know, Mom," he said, "if I was still a baby, I'd be crying right now."

Real Life—Real Laughs

I chuckled at his insight. He could have been angry and blamed me, but he chose self-reflection instead; I wished all adults could do that. He seemed awed to realize how much he had grown. I rejoiced at his ability to ponder his growth, an alignment with a greater perspective.

Sadly, when Jon was ten, my mom, his last and favorite grandparent, died. Jon and his grandma enjoyed mutual adoration, and I loved to see their affection for each other. The day after the sorrowful service, we flew home, and the plane encountered bumpy air. "Mom," Jon said, "there's so much disturbulence."

I smiled, amused at his made-up word, but not correcting him because I thought "disturbulence" perfectly described what we had gone through during the past week. Finding a word for deep feelings and sharing it with someone you trust starts a process of acceptance, paving the way toward equanimity. "Yes," I replied, "it's a whole lot of disturbulence."

At home that night, Jon crawled into bed. I scurried toward his room but passed his door, needing to set down papers in my nearby office before I tucked him in. I heard a plaintive little voice say, "Mom, aren't you going to come and put me to sleep?"

Having just returned from a funeral, I felt the dark humor of his words, "come and put me to sleep." I rushed into his room to kiss him goodnight, but I kept silent about his phrase. Luckily, in Jon's life, he hadn't yet experienced putting a pet to sleep; he seemed unfamiliar with another meaning for the term he used. At that moment, I focused only on his immediate needs. He craved the love and reassurance of a parent to comfort him in the evening's big transition into unconsciousness.

At age thirteen, John became a founding member of The Happy Club at school. The members exchanged jokes, positive news, songs, and stories. The group required each member to display a certain amount of happiness to maintain their membership. About a year later, Jon came home upset and I asked him why. "Mom," he moaned, "Stuart isn't happy. We've given him every chance to be happy at our meetings for the past few months, but he refuses every single time." Jon gulped and his eyes glistened. "Today, we had to drop him."

I commiserated, however inside, I couldn't help but imagine all the techniques the boys had probably used to cajole Stuart into jollity. Suddenly, I realized that Jon faced a serious emotional situation. I squared my shoulders and decided to address his reality as best I could.

"I'm so sorry," I said. "It sounds like you did everything possible for Stuart. I have found in my life that I can't always help everyone. It's really hard for me to accept that limitation."

Real Life—Real Laughs

I sympathized with Jon. Admitting what I could and couldn't do for people who I thought needed me in their illness, shortcomings, or pain remained one of my biggest soul challenges. Who would have thought I would face this through Jon's Happy Club?

At the end of the same school year, an excited Jon headed off to summer camp. At the last minute, he discovered he couldn't take any of his electronic gadgets with him. In my mind, I cheered the wise camp counselors. Jon lamented, "How will I survive without my favorite songs?" he asked me.

I shrugged. I had no idea.

Jon thought for a moment, then gushed forth with an idea. "I know. I'll take all the words to the songs with me in my mind. I'll sing them inside my head any time I want." He gave me a high five.

"Brilliant," I said. "That way, you always have your music with you wherever you go." It was a wonderful lesson for the spirit to find a way to calm and comfort himself, while keeping his mind filled with positivity instead of negative resentment. What a big step to realize he had this choice.

Right after college, Jon went to Japan with a good friend (who spoke Japanese). While I had very few qualms about the boys' abilities to take good care of themselves,

Real Life—Real Laughs

when I didn't hear from Jon for three days, I began to worry. Did he arrive okay?

Jon looked a lot like my dad who, tragically, passed away at age forty and never met my son. I remembered Dad fondly, for he often laughed at life's foibles. He loved to make beer in our basement and shared an abundance of this brew with nearby friends and family. I grew up thinking there was something wrong with neighbors' basements that didn't smell like hops. Whenever I worried about Jon, I mentally asked Dad for guidance. I figured the hereafter communication array must cover Japan; thus, I sent an urgent prayer to Dad, *Please look after Jon.*

The next day Jon texted me with a photo of himself at the Kyoto Octoberfest hoisting a beer stein. In that moment of grace, I laughed and immediately resonated with my father's warm and humorous presence, deeply reassuring me that Dad assisted Jon in the best way he knew how.

I have found that aligning with a higher power can be filled with comical, unexpected twists and turns. When I've been able to stay alert to this mindset, it has increased my gratitude, acceptance, self-reflection, meditation, grace, and transformation, just as it has for Jon.

Chapter 4
People Watching

James Haydn Kauffman Hite, **Kaethe Kauffman, Roman carvings 200CE, Turkey**, *photo, 2019*

Mom loved "people watching," as she called it. During my childhood, when sitting in a public place, she would poke me and giggle, "Look at that man's nose. It has a drop on the end. Oh, my God, it's about to drip." As we chuckled, we stared in suspense, waiting for the great event. When it fell at last, we collapsed into hysterics. Or she'd point out someone's unusual facial features, such as long earlobes. "People are fascinating," she would gush over the ears. I always agreed and her habit lived on in me after she died.

During those days, I don't remember her criticizing others; I absorbed an endless interest in people who I continued to observe. Becoming an artist, I drew, painted, and photographed close-ups of dancing feet, expressive hands, and moving muscles.

Like Mom, I stared at people while trying not to be creepy about it. In yoga class, while we twisted into a pose, then held it, I memorized the way other people's limbs crossed, and skin creased. When I went home, I drew what I remembered, life-sized.

I once spent two weeks on a trip with a beautiful Scandinavian tour guide whose ski-jump nose was so perky, her nostrils flared out and up at the end, as if she'd had an over-the-top Michael Jackson-type plastic surgery. I loved looking at her spectacularly large up-turned nostrils and wished I could show them to Mom.

Real Life—Real Laughs

In a recent large tour group in ancient ruins in rural Viet Nam, out in the jungle it became important to memorize unique characteristics of my group members. Luckily, I had years of experience doing that with Mom. One day, at jungle temples at My Son, I stopped to take photos of dancing demons carved into stone; I never could resist those types, whether on temple walls or in real life. After what seemed like a few moments of staring through the lens, I finished and looked around. The rushing guide with our group had completely disappeared and left me in thick forest. I scanned a distant group, but didn't find Mr. Orange, in a fluorescent embroidered t-shirt, or Lizard Eye, a cold reptilian type who I had asked, at an airport where she sat outside the ladies' room on a bench, if she could watch my carry-on bag while I used the facilities. With a flat stare, she had instantly replied, "No." At that moment, with trails diverging in four different directions in the dense green foliage, I would have loved to see Lizard Eye.

I had forgotten what panic felt like, as my stomach heaved upward, dangerously close to my mouth. I guessed that I stood about a mile from our bus. My sense of direction told me a deserted, twisting path on my right led to the coach, and I started off. But no one else trod that trail, so I changed my mind and reversed course. Happily, a kind woman recognized my fright and, with broken

English, asked if I was okay. Clearly, with my rolling eyes and wide gestures, I wasn't. I practically slavered with gratitude. With stuttering speech, I described my bus and her nice guide pointed me down the lonely, winding path on my right.

I reversed again, trotting off by myself. If only I could see Mr. Beef, who I had spotted on the deck of our ship one day on a lounge chair, splayed out in all his overweight, speedo-clad glory, reading a magazine that blared its title in large red font, "*BEEF.*" Mom would have adored him. I would have welcomed Ms. Mole with her large nose, pinched mouth and constant criticism. I wouldn't have minded following slow Ms. Wide Beam through crowds, one tiny step at a time.

The jungle, with squawking birds and probably slithering creatures lurking near me, proved to be a lonesome place. At the pace of my sweaty trot, I should have found my group by now. They, who traveled at the speed of the slowest cane-dependent members, clearly hadn't taken this path. I placed all my faith in the nice guide who had sent me in this direction. I hoped it wasn't his idea of a joke to direct lost tourists into a pit of hell. As an American in Viet Nam, I wouldn't have blamed him.

My faith proved well-placed. After a long half hour, I spotted the bus and, luckily, the group had not arrived yet. I lived in dread of holding up our travels with a silly mistake. When they arrived ten minutes later, none of them seemed to have missed me, including my guide. I felt too embarrassed to admit I had lost them. But inside, I was never so happy to see them all, even Lizard Eye.

In my gratitude, a dim thought entered. Categorizing or stereotyping someone by a single trait, the habit I had picked up from Mom, might be unkind. For example, Lizard Eye probably wasn't always forcing people to haul their roller bags into tiny Vietnamese toilet stalls, shared with resident lizards and frogs in several cases. Possibly, she had other fine qualities.

Like most things in life, watching people had its pros and cons. I could use my conscience to edit out mean streaks. I drew a deep breath and faced it; if I had said their nicknames aloud, Ms. Lizard Eye, Ms. Mole and Ms. Wide Beam would have suffered from my sarcastic tongue. I wouldn't do that again.

The yoga students I had drawn, Mr. Orange and even Mr. Beef would pass my personal integrity test. I could say their names out loud and not embarrass them or myself and enjoy guilt-free people-watching.

Chapter 5
Mom's Presence

Kaethe Kauffman, **Lost in Love***, collage, watercolor, 2014*

A few months ago, I cleaned out files and discovered I had kept 20 copies of my mother's obituary from 1999. I automatically recycle paper, putting documents with a

Real Life—Real Laughs

blank side into my printer: there I stowed fifteen extra copies of Mom's obituary. As I did so, I re-read the loving words and envisioned Mom, a sparkling extrovert. With her humor and witty opinions, she thrilled an audience, whether neighbors, family members, or her class of special education kids. It seemed that American art director Aaron Purmort knew Mom when he said, "She was known for her long, entertaining stories, which she loved to repeat often."

As I closed my printer, I sighed with the joy of recalling her and my grief at losing her. Busy with other things, I promptly forgot I had put her obituaries in the printer. But I continued to remember Mom.

At her memorial service, various folks took the mike and told Mom's favorite jokes, some of them a bit racy. We could have been a stand-up comedy club, except for the tears that mingled with laughter.

All my life, I strove to imitate Mom, because everyone adored her. However, as an introvert, I always preferred a good book to a group of people.

During the last three months, I prepared a speech for a local women's group. When I practiced, I recalled all I had learned from Mom: emote with enthusiasm, spice up facts with funny stories, smile, keep eye contact. The projected audience of 50 people made me very nervous.

When I at last stood at the podium and started my lecture, I trembled with fear. After I had turned the first page of my speech, I saw Mom's obituary on the back. And again, when I flipped the next page and the next.

I felt stunned and speechless for a moment. Then, a giggle arose, and I remembered Mom's style. Public speaker Jim Groth described Mom when he said, "She did not live an average life. She laughed inappropriately at every chance…"

I seemed to channel her charisma and genuinely enjoyed my give-and-take with audience members. At the end, I blushed at their excited ovation.

Mentally, I said, *Thanks, Mom*.

Chapter 6
In the Toilet

Kaethe Kauffman, **Author's Toilet**, *photo, 2024*

When I started dating slender, handsome Joe, I didn't suspect that our commode usage would come to mirror our relationship. While at his house, I flushed the toilet every time I used it. This must have galled my new boyfriend. But I didn't notice as I devoted myself to our infatuation and our love of yoga and hiking mountain trails.

After several months, at the point where neither of us minded if the other strolled into the bathroom at any time, I noticed that Joe didn't always flush. *No big deal,* I thought.

But he began to make surprising comments like, "Oh, so you're one of those flushers, wasting water." By this time, I had noticed he recycled each sliver of glass or plastic and composted every crumb. He had lived in Arizona and inexplicably decided that the jungle-like side of Oahu needed extreme water restriction measures.

"At home, I flush every third time unless I have company," I said, thinking this made me an eco-warrior. He sniffed and I guessed I hadn't seen the end of this topic. Luckily, Joe realized that Number Two required a flush. He allowed this renegade activity in a guest bathroom at the other end of the house.

When I accidentally flushed in his large bath, he gritted his teeth hard enough to alarm a dentist and muttered, "You've destroyed the Dilution Solution System." I didn't understand what he meant, but after that, I limited my occasional flushes to the faraway toilet.

One day Joe placed large pink plastic tubs in the shower stall. He complained that, at a shower's start, too much cool water escaped down the drain until the heat arrived. "At least one and one-half gallons of water are wasted," he declared. Used shower water eventually filled the rosy receptacles. When I peered into one, I saw grey scum on the surface. "Plants flourish with soapy grey water," he explained. Sure enough, his garden thrived with regular drenches from his tubs.

It took weeks before I felt brave enough to stand next to the huge pink tubs, strategically positioned to catch the most water. With shampoo blinding me at times, twice I stumbled and almost fell into them. I trained myself to remain rigid. After my first bathing success at his house, Joe grinned and said, "Oh, you showered this morning after I left for work. There's three more gallons for the plants." As we became closer, enjoying several yoga classes and hikes each week, he seemed pleased that I shared his environmental concerns. I felt glad to help with something important to him.

After four months, his scrawny eggplant twigs grew up to my chest and produced several mature vegetables. Joe found a recipe for baba ghanoush which we cooked together. It became a staple of our diet. His environmental efforts made a direct path from our sweaty water, through dark soil, up into the air, and then to our stomachs: life's miracles fully embodied.

Around this time, Joe allowed me to see toilet habits I had never imagined. Instead of using the handle to flush, he poured used water from the pink tubs into the toilet bowl, almost to the top. When I asked what he was doing, Joe mumbled, "Dilution is the solution to pollution" several times, as if reciting a mantra. Aha, the Dilution Solution System. When the water found its usual level again, the toilet, on its own, had completed the equivalent of a flush. Pee and bad smells dispersed, and gray water remained. A miracle! I had no idea toilets could be cleaned this way. Joe was a lavatory savant. We had achieved closeness as yogis, hiking partners and housemates. However, I noticed that our toilet-centered rebellion remained hidden from friends and visitors because, in my honest moments, it seemed a bit anti-social and possibly unsanitary.

Every few days, I hauled a pink tub out to the garden to douse the plants with their delicious dirty water. But hard as I tried, doing the same for the toilet repulsed me. Although I admired his non-flushing genius, this breach foreshadowed other cracks in our liaison.

When I repeated an amusing tidbit, he became annoyed. "I get it the first time. Just say it once," he growled.

Well, I thought, *we all have our buttons, and I pushed one of Joe's.* In my family tradition we retold favorite stories, reenforcing our common history. I tried to stop sharing choice items again but couldn't break the habit.

Real Life—Real Laughs

He thought my attempts at humor inane or, worse, insulting. I admit that telling him last year's Christmas saga of asking the teenagers among us to find someone in our condo building who would eat the leftover head of the roasted pig was probably insensitive to Joe's vegan lifestyle. Even though I wasn't as devoted a recycler, he would have approved of the tale's finale, had he stayed to hear it. The teens found neighbors who considered pig's head a special delicacy. "Great recycling," I had told them. With Joe, I gave up attempts at humor after this communication disaster.

In relationship give and take, why couldn't Joe tolerate the occasional repeated information in exchange for my embrace of his latrine habits? While this made sense to me, nevertheless, in yoga class, our tree poses wobbled as if blown by a gale. On every hiking day, it rained. Although I succeeded as a non-flusher of pee, our intimacy withered, unlike his enthusiastic eggplants. Six plump ones looked ready to harvest the day I left for good.

Just before I exited Joe's doorway the last time, with his complaints echoing in my ears, he thrust a quart jar of homemade baba ghanoush in my tote bag. Our comingled sweat had found this one fruition. It tasted rich and earthy, delightful.

Chapter 7
Conglomerate Catastrophe

I didn't expect life to get any better than the glorious travels I had recently enjoyed with my adult son, Jon. But the heights of my ecstasy apparently prompted a great master of the universe to take me down a few notches.

Upon arriving home, I couldn't have imagined the punch to my gut from a breast cancer diagnosis. Now I knew how a soccer ball felt at a soccer game: kicked and battered. Later, when I looked back, I realized my life had entered a period of complete reorganization, wholly without my permission.

After the first shock of diagnosis, I became aware that I had programmed my subconscious, for decades, by creating a long list of reasons why I would never get cancer. And I had truly believed them. When the doctor gave me the bad news, I wanted to shout at her, *But I'm vegetarian!* as if that exempted me from future illness.

I called Jon, who worked in Denver where he had attended college. I still lived in our condo in Honolulu where he grew up. I considered it a strength when his green eyes watered and sometimes overflowed during difficult times such as a break-up with a girlfriend or when our beloved pet cockatiel, Henry, got sick. When I told Jon the bad news, we both cried. He said he would be at my side for the surgery in six weeks. His support helped me begin to cope with my new reality.

I had never understood how humbling a potentially fatal disease felt. I became embarrassed at my former arrogance. I joined what I called "The Sisterhood" of wounded women like me. When I confided in friends about my health, I luxuriated in their sympathy. With their help, at last, I accepted my illness. All I had left to do was walk through the steps: surgery, radiation, and chemotherapy. With friends and Jon holding my hand, I could do this. I talked to Jon each week on the phone as we planned his trip home to Honolulu. His warmth and concern gave me great comfort.

In the six weeks between the diagnosis and the surgery, I caught up with bill-paying and emails and felt like life had resumed normal patterns. But all at once, my personal computer, Mabel, died. With no warning, she crashed and went into the shop for a ten-day overhaul, where her operating system would be removed and replaced by the latest version. I couldn't help but compare Mabel to my body going into the hospital for a similar procedure, to cut out the rot.

Despite this travail, I prided myself on retaining an optimistic, adapt-to-anything attitude. These set-backs were manageable, I told myself.

With Mabel on the fritz, I barely faltered in my workload. All Mabel's files were safe in the cloud. Life could proceed as normal, although at a slower pace with my travel lap-top, Betty, named for the elderly comic Betty White. I had depended on Betty the laptop for years while on the road. Although a slow poke, she got the job done.

But two days after living with the leisurely Betty, all internet browsers suddenly popped up messages that they wouldn't open on Windows XP anymore. I hadn't updated Betty's operating system because (it hurts me to think this, so I must mentally whisper it) Betty neared obsolescence and I didn't plan on updating her. I had put off a new purchase because Betty seemed indestructible. Fond of her, I knew all her lovable habits and foibles. And now Betty had keeled over. I began to grieve. "Not Betty, no, not Betty," I murmured as tears slipped down my cheeks.

After half a day of grieving, a long time for an aged laptop, I returned to work. With pluck, I put my chin up and turned to my last brain assistant that allowed me internet communication: my smart phone. Another dependable machine that had served me unstintingly for years, I kept Andy, short for Android, close to me always.

I could send texts and emails and manage my world for ten days until Mabel returned from the computer hospital. But, as if on cue from a secret plan hatched by a demon, the next day, Andy trembled and went blank, his battery fizzled. I shook my fists at the sky and yelled, "What? Et tu, Andy?"

At this point, I suspected larger malevolent forces at work. My head shook back and forth as I asked out loud. "Universe," I said, "you've lobbed another curveball. What the heck's going on?" I had no answer, but I continued to wonder. To get my work done, I trotted to Fed Ex to use their computers, teeth clenched together.

Yes, I understood I had babied Betty and Andy for too long. In a day or two, Andy bounced back, with a new battery. But I couldn't fully trust him anymore and didn't know how to use Andy to write the essays I needed for my work. The unappealing Fed Ex computers sat in a refrigerated, sterile environment with the meter clicking at thirty-five cents a minute. The spoiled web-dependent part of me stamped her foot at the great injustices served up all at once: body failure and three layers of back-up brain function blitzed out.

Festering with anger, I completed Elizabeth Kubler Ross's five stages of dealing with major trauma. I had denied, bargained, grieved, and accepted my devices' and my body's breakdowns. Life as I'd known it had disappeared. However, my machines hadn't finished their mutinies yet. The creepiest one had yet to perish.

The next day, I heard a strange sound as I walked past my bathroom. "Brrrrrr-brrrrrr." I rushed into the room to see my electric toothbrush, Mr. Grin, dancing on his charger. Surely, I hadn't forgotten to turn him off. I pushed the turn-off button. There. Quiet. But one-half hour later, I heard "Brrrrrr" again. How could that be? This time, I handled Mr. Grin gingerly, afraid he might explode. I took him off the charger in case the apparatus, with its lithium battery, might send sparks up the stem. To be extra safe, I unplugged the charger before I left the house, sure that all would be well.

Happily, Jon arrived in Honolulu from Denver for my impending surgery. As it turned out, he also did damage control with Mabel, Betty, and Andy. But when I got home that day Jon said, "Mom, Mr. Grin has lost his dentifrice mind. He's shaking all over the counter, making a racket."

"Oh dear," I said, "I'm afraid it's Toothbrush Dementia. Would you google a cure?" We discovered no remedy. Much to our horror, Mr. Grin's gristly fits continued into the next day. Finally, the last flicker of electricity left him lifeless, sprawled on the bathroom counter. I shuddered and quickly rejected the thought that he might be a premonition.

Oddly, Jon's electric toothbrush, Mr. Toothy, quietly passed away with somber dignity the night before my surgery. They had been purchased together, and their names bonded them as the Misters Toothy Grin.

These electronic deaths seemed more than coincidental. I had read that strong emotions can trigger psychic events. I had to admit cancer brought up a fear of death. Although I wasn't tearing my hair or beating my chest, I felt like a carpet had been pulled out from under my feet. I thought I had faced my fears and avoided denial by talking honestly to friends, Jon and spiritual counselors. I didn't need electronic collapse to illustrate my situation. Apparently, a Higher Power disagreed.

A spiritually attuned friend told me that major electric disorders meant one thing: someone on the other side was desperately trying to contact me. But I knew of no dead people who would want to talk to me, which made me feel a little pathetic. We are all supposed to have kindly loved ones watching over us from the great beyond. The only grandmother I had known had a permanent frown etched on her silent face and she terrified me. Besides, it was too late to warn me I had cancer. I already knew the worst. And if a more distant ancestor in the spirit world wanted to tell me I would be okay, why would he or she yank my electronic support systems, which made my life worse? The spirit world didn't make sense. For comfort, I went back to my bedrock meditation routine, morning and evening, with prayers.

Amidst this domestic mechanical mayhem, Jon drove me to the hospital for surgery on a sunny fall day at 5:30 a.m. Luckily, it hadn't occurred to me that the sudden death of four of my most intimate pieces of equipment might signify a curse on the cancer surgery. If Jon had doubts, he wisely kept them to himself.

Aside from removing cancer from my body, the best thing about surgery proved to be the pure joy I felt when I woke up and found Jon at my side. He offered ice chips to my parched tongue. They helped dispel what felt like a mouth filled with gasoline fumes, apparently the taste of anesthesia. He gently drove me home. Not the most skilled nurse, he didn't spoil me with plumped pillows, meals and hot tea. But he expressed his love by rescuing my pieces of equipment, providing a huge relief.

While I recovered from surgery, Jon bought a new Betty, the same kind of tablet he had, and an updated Android like his, making it easy to consult with him about future electronic issues. He had originally built Mabel from scratch, and I relied on my techie son to keep me electronically viable. Next, he helped start and/or re-install all the programs I needed on Mabel and the rest of my brain partners. He lessened the confusion and grief of a sea-change, and restored equanimity. Post-surgery and electronic melt-down, I endured, bruised and damaged, but cancer-free and data-complete.

Perhaps Jon and I inherited a pioneer resilience from my immigrant ancestors. They had left all they knew, traipsed to strange territory and established new homes. I mentally thanked my great-grandparents for their courage.

In my cancer journey, I emerged humbled, but healthy, with new varieties of Mabel, Betty, and Andy. Jon purchased a well-behaved Mr. Grin for me and a sparkling white Mr. Toothy for himself. As happened on the trip to our ancestral homes, my son and I found ourselves once again spiritually aligned in our affection, ancestry, electronics, and tooth-cleaning machines.

Chapter 8
Giant Jiminy and Mr. Clean

Kaethe Kauffman, **Musical Fire**, pastel, pencil, 7"x10", 2024

After I completed eight months of cancer treatments in Honolulu, I craved a celebration. Many hours of meditation, prayer, and great support from professionals and friends got me through the ordeal.

Three close friends agreed to join me on my five-day vacation in Las Vegas. I had carefully scheduled their visits and created a master plan. My buddies, after decades of deep comradeship through all of life's turmoil, would stay two days each with slight overlaps. Joan planned to drive from Reno, eight hours on the road. Joel lived one and one-half hours away in a small desert town. Cecily had a home in Las Vegas but overwhelmed with her divorce, would pop in whenever she could.

Having run the gauntlet of surgery, radiation, and chemotherapy, I deserved a resounding reunion with my dearest friends. Cancer had slapped me down. One day, I walked around leading a normal life. The next day, I became a "cancer patient," a bizarre new identity. But if you must have cancer, Hawaii is the place to get it. In the warm winter breezes, I took daily long walks, savoring the sun and ocean. I deepened my Buddhist faith in the nearby temple. The cancer doctors gave me a 90 percent survival rating, the same odds I faced whenever I crossed the street. Glory hallelujah.

For many years, every few months, I returned to Nevada. I had developed a deep reverence for the hiking trails and for my Nevada friends. Each time I met my desert cronies, we updated each other with the new insights we had gained about our lives. I needed a party with good giggle sessions, a great cure-all according to Norman Cousins and other medical experts.

Cancer got a bad rap, but in my case, it proved to be the atom bomb of all motivators. I refused to put up with

Real Life—Real Laughs

anyone's disrespect because ecstatic life sparkled around me like a sea of exquisite jewels. I visualized my personal cancer-destroying agent as Mr. Clean, the smiling bald cartoon man who advertised household cleanser. He held strong opinions about scrubbing negativity out of life: scour away bad situations and turn toward life-giving joy.

During my childhood years, I memorized the songs of my favorite cartoon character, Jiminy Cricket. His musical refrain, *"And always let your conscience be your guide,"* had rung through my mind for six decades, making him a giant among crickets. At the earliest age, his ethos took root in me. My Jiminy Cricket-inspired conscience told me I needed to take good care of myself first, a new concept for me.

Now Jiminy Cricket and Mr. Clean joined together. These two powerhouses fused to become a super-hero I called Giant Jiminy, helping me focus on joyful healing. With an enormous cricket at the helm, I became determined to create a happy vacation week. I felt as if I had planted a flag atop a personal mountain, stating, *I claim laughter in my name.*

Bring on my Jolly Crew, as I mentally called them: Joan, Cecily, and Joel. *All will go well*, I thought, until Joan told me her husband, Ned, had a conflict and couldn't come to Las Vegas. I might have expected this, for Joan and her wonderful spouse did everything together and, unfortunately, like thousands of others, Ned hated Tinsel Town. I understood. Over the years, I had met the stereotyped Las Vegans Ned talked about: the down-and-outs, gamblers, and alcoholics.

Whenever I felt discouraged by Sin City's disreputable side, desert magic overpowered casino slime every time. When I inhaled the sweet and musty smell of rain on arid sand and sage, I became re-intoxicated. I bathed in the crisp air and vibrant light and couldn't get enough of them. The ever-changing shapes of cloud shadows on the mountains surrounding the town entranced me. The mega-sized shadows seemed to embrace me when I hiked into mountain canyons. Year after year, I continued my love affair with Nevada's arid wonders.

For my five-day vacation, I could rely on Cecily and Joel. But Cecily, fighting in the trenches of her divorce, had hired three people to help her prepare copious documents for a looming deadline. I could only meet with her for one dinner, and I appreciated even that amount of time. I felt proud of her. She had built a solid support team as she slogged through her third year of separation from a difficult husband.

Surely Joel would come through for me. We had been good friends for three decades, and our sons were the same age. We always tried to outdo each other with corny jokes, just what the doctor ordered. Over the years, Joel had confided in me about his semi-open marriage where he maintained monogamy with a wandering third wife. A few years ago, when his third marriage began to have trouble, he also took a new demanding job that limited our visiting time.

I had not seen him in several months. He had texted that he would be available on my party dates. I looked forward to seeing him. I could use a few dozen jokes. But, at the last minute, he had to work and couldn't make it. I felt let down and hoped his job wasn't running him ragged. When he had an unhappy home life, he tended to overwork.

Giant Jiminy came to the rescue, tapping his red umbrella on the floor as he chirped, "C'mon Cate, is your focus on Joel and his troubles making you a happier person and killing cancer cells?"

"No, Giant Jiminy," I humbly replied. He had a way of clarifying the murk. I mentally left Joel to his own confusing life.

Now I faced an empty five days with my plans in tatters. I had expected riotous fun and a warmly fulfilling time with my devoted group, only to find a vast and unexpected silence around me instead. At first, I grabbed the phone to call more friends, to fill the blank space with hilarious personalities for the extraordinary celebration I craved. But I put the phone down. I stared at it instead and savored the delicious quiet. I sighed, calmer.

After a day of walking in the desert, amazed by the brilliant magenta cactus flowers, I opted for introverted peace. I picked a bouquet of orange, blue, and white wildflowers (the non- prickly kind) and felt the full glory of such beauty. Every afternoon, I made fires in my living room fireplace and gazed at them for hours, mesmerized by their soft burbling language, as if they explained secrets of meditation to me and I understood. When I felt a soft connection to the divine, I took the time to pray. I said *thank you* for my health. Over the week, I gained a gentle strength.

I read funny books and laughed out loud. With no schedule and no demands, I finally installed a toilet paper holder in the bathroom, a job I had avoided for five years. I realized I had unconsciously assumed a boyfriend or my adult son would put it up someday. Peacefully, I hauled out my drill, studied the directions and completed the task in an hour. Even though someone more experienced would have done it in five minutes, I didn't curse my slowness. Instead, I let pride flow through me.

A couple of days later, I transformed a hallway wall leading to my bathroom into a rogues' gallery, hanging framed family photos from my grandparents onward: the pioneers, the self-educated, the inebriated, the award-winning pie-makers, the workaholics, and the crooks. To complete the cycle, I added photos of my son and me. All the family gathered, revered on my wall, despite our imperfections.

Days of nun-like wandering under the spring desert sun soothed my spirit. I made a new pal during my unusual span of free time: me.

I bid cancer cells an official farewell with every wildflower I savored, with the fires I built, the prayers I said, the gratitude I felt, the family photos I hung, each belly laugh, and each swath of toilet paper I unfurled. Simple life became my sacred vacation while I learned to honor myself as my own best friend.

My buddies had ditched me and also blessed me, giving me the gift of bountiful inner space. Being kind to myself, moment by moment, became my new way to party. Thank you, friends. Bless you, Giant Jiminy.

My mind's eye saw the colossal cricket lift his extra-large blue top hat and nod his head at me with a smile. I blew him a kiss.

Chapter 9
Zero Testosterone

Kaethe Kauffman, **Deep Rest,** photo, 2022

I didn't miss my testosterone until it disappeared. A year ago, doctors discovered a small malignancy in my breast that ate hormones for breakfast, lunch, dinner, and dessert. After surgery and radiation, my main job became reducing the threatening estrogen and testosterone down to zero.

I have always been a gung-ho person, chasing goals, eager to catch them. Even though I had never graced the cover of *TIME* magazine, I couldn't help trying. Perhaps I was born with racehorse genes and needed to reach the finish line. More likely, I kept trying to impress a critical mother. In retrospect, I realized these huge efforts required a cornucopia of testosterone. Women average 15 to 60 nanograms per deciliter (ng/dL) of testosterone, enough to work, bear and raise children and keep our communities together. I probably ran on 70-plus ng/dL.

Luckily, with the help of a local doctor, Dr. Alcott, I found natural supplements that did the trick, bringing me down to a healthy—for me—seven ng/dL. She also helped me with psychological tweaking. Dr. Alcott taught me that testosterone increases during conflicts. For a few months, I hung out with a contrarian boyfriend who doled out sarcastic judgments that sparked me into bickering with him. During this time, my testosterone levels rose from seven ng/dL to 50 ng/dL, even while taking the hormone-lowering supplements. After our break-up, my hormones plunged to zero. This graphic lesson persuaded me to keep my life calm.

I now resembled a happy walking zombie, so relaxed that events felt as if they moved like molasses. Hormone inertia made me contemplate my every move four or five times, whether going to the gym or the bathroom, things that used to be habits. No longer tantalized by a looming goal, never leaping up to race somewhere or debate with someone, I hardly recognized the new me. Being Jello-girl felt okay for a while. But I came to realize I needed to talk to people, work, and exercise, very difficult for gelatin to do.

I had a serious talk with myself. *Self*, I said, *I'm a survivor. Could this strange slowness become okay in some way? Perhaps it's merely a new phase of life. I've completed different stages of development before.*

Remembering as far back as I could, I realized I had navigated difficult challenges throughout life: crawling, later walking (a big deal at the time), next running, puberty (AAAARGH), pregnancy, childbirth, breastfeeding (harder than childbirth), tough relationships, a career, child-rearing, various surgeries, illnesses, and menopause.

When I looked at this list, my shoulders squared with pride at how much I had achieved. Nothing had come easily. Grit had always been my best friend in life's endurance race. Maybe I could let myself be satisfied and give up the need to strive.

After menopause, I thought I would be on Easy Street, a happy semi-retiree with no more transformations until the big "D" at the end of life. I hoped to die in my sleep like my grandmother had, during her post-Thanksgiving dinner nap. But between menopause and D-

Day (or T-Day if I was as lucky as Grandma), I assumed I would catch a break, a nice long one.

Checking my list, I saw that the loss of estrogen and testosterone paled by comparison with other giant life changes. I could do this. But I found it hard to achieve the basics in life. In my hormone-less state, I lacked motivation and energy. In my previous life, I had always enjoyed automatic gumption. I needed a strategy. Perhaps I could create artificial determination to make up for the absent testosterone. Like artificial insemination and artificial intelligence, maybe it would work.

I began a program of inner pep talks. Being a morning person, I focused on how wonderful I would feel after an early workout at the gym. I imagined the good tingling of happy muscles. My body bought into the idea, and I sped out the door first thing. After a few times, the new routine overcame my hormone-less lassitude.

Scheduling work, volunteer jobs, and social events on my calendar provided an automatic kick in the pants. In my mind, the almighty calendar must be obeyed.

I could accomplish a skeleton version of my former life. I sighed. Honestly, I preferred the ego puffery I had enjoyed with a full titer of testosterone when I automatically dashed around accomplishing all that pleased me. But that life no longer remained an option. I kept reminding myself that calm brought real happiness, especially with the lack of cancerous tumors that went along with low hormones.

I needed to honor my new ability to easily relax and savor the moment, free from the modern American obsession to prove self-importance with a hectic schedule. Gradually, I discovered advantages to my slow-floating world.

I took time to meditate, read, and dream, and began to savor these precious hours every day. My mantra became, *Testosterone free, the way to be*. As a tribute to my inner Jello, I came to love the Vibra-Shake Power Plate machine at the gym where I passively stood while the foot platform shuddered. Every fat cell and water molecule quivered like Santa's tummy when he laughed. Being a quaking blob turned out to be surprisingly delightful.

Chapter 10
I Am More Mature Than That

Kaethe Kauffman, **Male Dancer Blue,** *charcoal, pastel, 12"x9", 2012*

Real Life—Real Laughs

Some people got to see naked men free, like my friend Diane. Other people did not, like me. It was a simple fact of life, not a cosmic conspiracy, so I told myself. In most conflicts, I thought I behaved like a mature adult, until I looked around and noticed an inner adolescent acting out without my permission.

Nothing challenged my sense of maturity like the subject of men, naked or otherwise. In Japan, my tour group enjoyed natural hot springs in a remote mountain village; boys on one side of a small hill, girls on the other. The Japanese tradition was strict nudity in the onsen, or hot springs. However, Diane decided to take a walk up a bordering river in a public area outside the onsen boundary, where all hikers were clothed. From there she discovered she could view the men walking around in their separate hot springs enclave, wearing only their birthday suits.

Naturally, for the rest of our visit to this bucolic country town, I traipsed up and down the river many times, searching for nude men. Did I see one? No. And I kicked almost 100 rocks as hard as I could, venting over this unfairness. Why did Diane get so lucky? But eventually, it occurred to me that I could be a mature person and accept the universe's decision that Diane got to see men in the raw and I did not. But I became obstinate, bordering on obsession, like a gambler; this time

I would get lucky. I continued to wear a deep path along that river. Ms. Inner Teen-Ager did not give up easily.

As life does, the universe threw me other opportunities to consider my maturity level. A recent charity fundraiser on Valentine's Day requested all women to wear pink. I hated pink, a bubble-gum and teeny-bopper color. Society painted femininity as pink, frivolous and mindless. As an artist who viewed colors objectively in their constantly changing contrasts to each other, I should be more mature. In the great prism of the visible spectrum, pink was an innocent color. Perhaps I should have used pink in my art the way nature used it in her palette: natural rose tints at sundown and sunrise, the warm glow of sandstone and quartz. But I remained prejudiced against the blameless color. At the fundraiser, I caved in to social pressure and forced myself to wear pink. But I shuddered all evening, assuming people considered me to be a silly young girl. Objectively, my anger at pink seemed to be an unnecessary lack of self-worth.

Even with this evidence to the contrary, I still considered myself a confident and worldly person, tolerant and amused at most human foibles. However, I could not ignore the evidence that, besides relationships with men, my family members adroitly decimated my inner poise at times.

Real Life—Real Laughs

When my beloved Aunt Fiona died, I immediately traveled 2,500 miles to be with my cousins who had lost their mother. I assumed I would find a motel or hotel nearby, but they insisted I sleep in their mom's house with several of them. Caught up in shock and grieving, I forgot that my dear cousins were terminal practical jokers and, as kids, I had often been their target. Flattered by their thoughtfulness and wanting to help as much as I could with the memorial service, I welcomed the chance to be closer to them. They showed me to a pleasant bedroom with treasured family photos I had never seen before on the wall: our grandparents and my sadly deceased father. He was Aunt Fiona's only sibling, and they had been close.

I should have been suspicious. My cousins were being far too kind. For some reason, I spent a lot of time asleep. Throughout my several days' stay, each night I sank into a divinely profound, dreamless, and long slumber.

As my five female cousins tried to reconcile their diverse new-age religious beliefs to take care of their mother after her death, I eventually learned that one cousin insisted the body should not be moved for two days. It being summer, Aunt Fiona had been packed in ice for informal viewings and prayer vigils. But no one had considered rigor mortis. By the time the "two-day rule" cousin relented and allowed Aunt Fiona to go to a mortuary, she was so stiff, no one could get her out the narrow bedroom door. No one thought to google "rigor mortis" where they could have learned it would naturally end by day three. Instead, they removed the picture window of the bedroom to lift her out. She only fell once.

All of this happened, and the window was repaired, before I arrived. I smiled and shrugged when I heard several versions of it; this constituted normal activity on my father's side of the family. At the beautiful memorial service, my aunt's opera student granddaughter sang a goosebump-raising lullaby from Beethoven that had us all in tears, a fine tribute.

When I said farewell to my cousins, one casually mentioned that I had slept in my aunt's bedroom, in fact, in the bed where she breathed her last, including the plastic wrapped mattress where ice chunks allowed her to lie in state for days. My cousins had put me there because every other relative refused to sleep in that bed. I felt heat in my jaws and cheeks crawl up my face in irritation.

During childhood, I had been the family fall guy when they sent me running to a far pasture to bridle the horse when they knew the horse contently noshed on her hay in the nearby barn. Or they told me they would meet me at the river "that way," they said, pointing. "You go ahead, we'll run in the kitchen and grab some lemonade and meet you there." When I traipsed off alone, I soon found myself in a field with the giant scary bull and no cousins in sight.

I reminded myself that my victimhood days were gone. My fingers twitched with the desire to throw a cousin on the bed to see how she liked it. My powerful inner teenager would love it; I could feel her evil grin urging me on.

Then I thought of Aunt Fiona. I had slept like the dead in her bed, a wonderful gift in my sometimes-insomniac world. And I could almost see my aunt slapping her thigh with laughter. In her name, I gulped anger down, decided to rise above the occasion, and refrained from physically mauling my cousins. Maturity seemed to dictate that I silence my restless teenager who wanted revenge for this insult plus the times they pushed me in the lake and locked me in the goat pen with the horned butting beasts. But the next time someone died at home, I would make sure to know which fated bed it happened in.

Just as Ms. Teen-Ager did not give up searching for naked men while she walked up and down the Japanese river bordering the onsen hot springs, so she didn't give up on me now. Before, I had thought her determination to get the same visual treats as Diane in Japan, her hatred of pink, and her anger at my cousins' practical jokes were immature. But now, I accepted my inner teenager's fiery zeal and strength as part of my maturity.

Real Life—Real Laughs

Real Life—Real Laughs

Part Two

Friends?

James Haydn Kauffman Hite, **Kaethe Kauffman & Whiskers, Haida Gwaii, Canada,** *photo, 2014*

Chapter 11
The Seal Who Loved My Sister

I never envied my older sister, Marlene, until a handsome seal fell in love with her and not me. While kayaking in the Queen Charlotte Islands in western Canada, a group of friendly seals suddenly surrounded us. After five or ten minutes, the one pictured above stayed near while the others wandered off. The seal came close to me and communed for a few minutes. As the photo reveals, I warmly welcomed it, gushing about its beauty. But flattery didn't work. It turned away and swam to my son, in his mid-twenties. The big-eyed, long-whiskered mammal ventured close and gazed at my young, strong offspring. At that moment, I named the seal Whiskers. It promptly left to visit Marlene's kayak. With striking high cheekbones and long blond hair, my sister had always been a beauty.

I love Marlene, but, like many siblings, we haven't had the easiest relationship. We grew up in a combative and competitive household where I could never forget that I held the lowest position. Eight years older than me, Marlene seemed like another adult: big, loud, and superior. And more dangerous. My parents rarely employed corporal punishment on me, other than an occasional spanking. But a sibling had no such restraint. If our parents looked away, I could expect shoves, spitball strikes and being tripped and sent sprawling.

Like my parents, Marlene maintained an extroverted command over those around her. Sadly, she inherited Mom and Dad's weight problems. As an adult, Marlene celebrated when the scale stayed below three hundred pounds. But, often, it didn't. This broke my heart, both for my parents and my sister. My father died of a heart attack at age forty, so we all remained hyper-aware of the health hazards of being overweight. For some odd reason, undue weight gain never bedeviled me. Vicariously experiencing my family's diet agonies over the years, I felt deeply grateful at my surprising dissimilarity.

Regardless of size, our family always loved the outdoors. Camping and hiking were our favorite activities. Marlene enjoyed inexhaustible strength in the wilderness. That's why I invited her to join us kayaking in Canada, even though she'd reached her seventy-first year.

Because of her weight, the kayak sat low in the water, the black line running around the rim submerged. Perhaps that's why Whiskers favored her. It could get closer to her than to my son and I, who bobbed farther above the water line. Perhaps Marlene's overall body shape resembled a seal and Whiskers felt a kinship. I tried to refrain from mentally applying the epithet, "blubber," highly esteemed by ocean mammals, but not so much by humans. I imagined I felt only compassion for Marlene's affliction. I thought I had rejected our family tradition of name-calling and mean teasing, but perhaps I hadn't. That I used this word, even silently, made my cheeks heat up with shame. Later I was informed by a nephew that I am excused from guilt due to a principle called sibling payback.

For whatever reason, Whiskers stuck to Marlene, swimming around and around her, and under the small boat, to pop up on the other side. With its sharp barks, Whiskers might have been laughing. Much to our amazement, it began to propel her vessel by pushing it from behind. Next, it glided up to the bow and shoved the side with its nose, first on one side and then the other, effectively turning the boat this way and that. All of us giggled at the seal's antics. Whiskers remained persistent, seeming to flirt with my sister.

I grew jealous. What did Whiskers see in Marlene that it didn't see in me? I wanted the seal to fall in love with me instead of her. Our eight-year age difference meant we never wanted to date the same guys. Until now.

I called out, "Hey, Whiskers, come over here, boy." It didn't even glance at me. The seal had made up its mind and remained devoted to Marlene. The sprightly animal swam to Marlene's side, giving little barks and nipping at her kayak. We continued to chuckle at the seal, perceiving no danger. It never occurred to us that my sister, a tough lady, should be cautious around a cute, pesky sea mammal. But we underestimated Whiskers.

After playing at Marlene's side for ten minutes or so, at last, it seemed to make a decision, *Enough of this courtship, it's time for a bold move.* All at once, with great flaps of its tail and flippers, it leapt into the kayak, its head landing in Marlene's lap. Whiskers teetered on the rim, its back-end wiggling in the air, as if trying to push its whole body onto Marlene.

Marlene yelled, "What the hell?" She picked up her oar and began shoving the seal with it. Whiskers might have been a boyfriend who had gone too far and needed boundaries. The two tussled for a few minutes as more expletives and barks flew through the air. Tall for a woman, at five feet nine inches, Marlene proved to be a good match for Whiskers, who looked to be about six or seven feet long, from nose to outstretched tail-flippers. Their body weights may have been comparable. With her kayak low in the water, Marlene provided substantial ballast, keeping her craft stable. At last, the animal seemed to comprehend Marlene's rejection and Whiskers slowly slid back into the water. A fierce glare from my sister's furrowed brow followed the chastised seal. "That's right, keep away from me," she called out to Whiskers, who, nonetheless, stayed nearby.

Now, it might turn to me, I thought, hopeful. But Whiskers kept its eyes on Marlene, although it didn't attempt to jump in her kayak again. Boundary setting could apparently work with over-eager guys of all species.

Whiskers swam near Marlene as we slowly kayaked back to camp, and they began speaking again. I heard her mummer, "Hey there, you're all right as long as you stay in the water. Don't get me wrong, you're a good-looking guy."

The faithful animal gave low grunts and affectionate nose pushes to the side of her vessel. We saw its clan at a distance, playing in the water. When we neared the shore, Whiskers gave a last bark and swam away to join its group. My sister and the seal seemed to part on good terms.

Our family still laughs about Whiskers falling in love with Marlene, but, secretly, I wish it could have been me.

Chapter 12
Henry IV

Kaethe Kauffman, **James Bird Showering**, *photo, 2018*

At home, when I have called out, "Henry!" four heads would swivel my way in unison. But only one of them knows my secrets.

I consider myself an honest person and freely answered everything my partner, Henry I, asked and more. But soon after we moved in together, he seemed to stop wondering about me: short honeymoon. As much as I tried to engage him in titillating details about our lives, including news about friends and family, he remained distant. Had he heard me say that a niece was pregnant again or that a nephew was back in rehab? Silence. I don't like to hoard secrets.

As our child, Henry II, grew older, I realized that all the confidences I bestowed in him as a baby dwindled. Friends told me they were amazed by how much Henry II and I talked to each other, even during his teen-age years. They often asked what my secret was. Non-plussed, I said, "I just ask him questions, and for some unknown reason, he answers."

But there are natural and societal barriers to full confidence between a parent and child. At age fifteen, as we stood in the wreckage of our family, he politely yet emphatically requested not to hear negative details about his dad. I wanted my son to enjoy the best possible relationship with his father, so I said to him, "I'll respect and honor your request." I used formal language to make it sound serious. And I have tried my best to do so.

However, we would happily discuss food and cooking, his girlfriends, my mostly non-existent boyfriends, his social groups of friends and mine, our apartment issues, our jobs, our sports, and our ethics concerning difficult situations. In his twenties at his first job, he struggled. "Mom, when the boss is gone for the day, everyone in the office takes a few extra hours at

Real Life—Real Laughs

lunch. How do I avoid being a goody two-shoes when I don't want to go with them?" We explored possible solutions. I relish these interesting talks.

We also discuss forgiveness. "Yeah, with my first girlfriend, I used doormat forgiveness. It didn't work. She just kept on taking advantage of me."

"I get it. I did the same thing for years," I told him. "What kind of forgiveness do you use now?"

"Something that feels true for me, and not just to get her off my case."

I laughed, pleased. "Makes sense to me." Despite our gaps, we remain close in most of life's subjects.

In the same way, with added limitations, Henry III was a constant delight. He was a chatty neighbor boy who, because of difficulties with his parents which we don't discuss, spent much of his childhood in our home. Henry III has been Henry II's best friend since kindergarten and like a second son to me. The two looked so much alike during their childhood, they were constantly mistaken for brothers. Both brunette, Henry II has hazel eyes and number three has brown, the only major distinction.

Henry III was as open as translucent book pages that flap in the wind. Precociously verbal and a serious reader, even in kindergarten, he and Henry II (mostly a non-reader of books) nevertheless bonded like baby birds in a nest. As the boys grew to adulthood, I respected their teen-age secrets, except when one of the boys got a little drunk. But even with inebriation, I avoided probing into their private lives.

Now age 27, Henry III has lived in Japan for five years. But when he comes home to visit, we endlessly gossip about school friends, cultural differences between the US and Japan, weight loss and gain (a surprisingly popular topic with young men), hairstyles on face and head, jobs, reading, and social trends. He's a hoot and we laugh a lot. I dearly love my boys but respect the boundaries we've set.

The next Henry to walk into my life, Henry IV, is the one who knows my secrets. He's a bright banana yellow cockatiel and we immediately fell in love. One day, when Henry II and III were six, playing outside, they spied a miniature parrot (about ten inches high) walking toward them in a stately manner. We later learned it was a cockatiel. Quickly the boys discovered it was tame and they brought the bird home. We fashioned a small, crude enclosure for it. We lived in a rental house with no pets allowed, so I called the landlady and begged to keep the bird, since it had, almost literally, walked into our home. Surprisingly, she acquiesced.

Henry IV had brilliant orange cheeks. He was a loud friendly fellow who looked you in the eye and understood the rhythm of language: I talked, he replied or

Real Life—Real Laughs

vice versa. Many humans don't know this essential rhythm to communication. With his steady gaze and his leaning-toward-me body language, the bird seemed to understand when I talked to him.

Within hours, our bird imprinted on my son, Henry II, and me. Henry III got called home and missed the critical imprinting period. This meant that our new cockatiel perched on our fingers, rode on our shoulders, crawled around on our anatomy as one of us laid on the couch, played games with us, rough sometimes with a six-year-old Henry II, but both seemed to thrive. Much to Henry I's chagrin, the bird always ran away from him. I don't know if birds limit their imprints to two other beings, or if Henry IV has better instincts than me when it comes to family member selection.

The Henrys dithered for days about what to call the bird, assuming he was a male. They tossed around cutesy names like Big Bird, or Snarky or White Fang. But none of them stuck. After three days, I declared, "We must call him something." They agreed. With a flash of inspiration, I called out, "Henry!" Four heads pivoted in my direction, and we had our name. Now I needed to say only one word to rivet four males to my attention. Life is sweet.

Twenty years ago, bird books defined cockatiels with bright orange cheeks as males. Nowadays, science has determined more subtle gender characteristics which would make our bird a female, but we didn't know that at the time.

Henry IV loved to talk to me about anything, day or night, unlike Henry I. My avian Henry and I didn't seem to have any boundaries to conversation, unlike Henrys II and III. When no one else was home, I spilled everything; Henry IV's sparkling eyes, head nodding at the right places and conversational repartee in perfect rhythm made me feel certain I was understood. We both seemed to gain enormous satisfaction from our exchanges, even though we spoke different languages.

After our discovery that Henry IV was female, a family vote kept her name as Henry. She didn't nest nor lay eggs, and she was as rascally and rambunctious as an ADHD teen-age boy with an excess of testosterone. Because she was gender ambivalent, we took care to explain to her that in our household, we do not discriminate against gender fluidity. We fully accepted her just as she was.

In our serious and ambitious world, Henry IV and I secretly shared how much we love to laugh and play. Adults don't do this often unless drinking, watching sports, TV, a movie comedy, or participating in an organized class such as tap dance. My bird Henry and I laughed, sang, and fooled around every day. I taught her hula: she switched her tail back and forth and spread her

Real Life—Real Laughs

wings while nodding her head as she watched me dance the Hukilau. She taught me bird ballet: one wing (on me it's an arm) and leg fully extended for a graceful moment, then switch in rhythm to the other side.

We made up songs about our daily adventures, the main one being a happy dance: we would bob around with chirps (her) and me belting out, "The waves are so big, shining turquoise and pounding and I'm so happy, I got that chapter done." I can't think of a human friend I could do this with, except for a young child.

But Henry IV understood something even more essential than fun to me: stillness. Americans love to be busy. Even among my retired friends, the busier one is, the more prestige one gains. I would never admit to friends or family how severely immobile I am for a good part of each day. If my doctor knew, he'd give me Prozac. However, with enough quietude, joy bubbles through me and I bounce up, eager for escapades with friends. My dear bird, Henry, understood me better than my doctor, for with Henry IV, I could share my true introvert colors. The more I stayed home with her, the happier she was. She knew how quiet I could be. She was the only soul who knew how much I meditated, often with her on my shoulder two to three hours, sometimes more each day.

Cockatiels sleep, or transcend to birdie meditation realms, twelve hours out of every twenty-four, so I found my soul mate in Henry IV. She was content to ride my meditation aurora borealis with me. The moment I drifted to the surface from meditation, she started chirping. Time to dance and sing again. Modern culture is very noisy; it seems life has become louder by the decade, as if to prove how much more important this era is than the last. It now feels un-American to be quiet with no TV or radio blaring. I must be a tiny minority who craves silence for hours each day, like an essential nutrient. With a quota of calm under my belt, I can race around working, running errands, and doing volunteer work with the best of them, thoroughly enjoying each minute I share with the multitudes.

As an adult, my son, Henry II, works in another state, is stimulated by his job, and grateful to be climbing the corporate ladder. I couldn't be prouder of him. We are in close contact. Also devoted to Henry IV, he related to her as if she were his brother/sister-of-the-heart.

When Henry IV had a serious illness, on a particularly bad day, Henry II was so alarmed, he jumped on a midnight plane, emailing his boss that he had to be with his only pet for the last twenty years. For a week, he cared for Henry IV while doing his job via computer. He said his boss understood.

Luckily, my son doesn't see his mother as a pathetic person depending on a silly bird to be her best friend.

Henry IV is a bona fide family member with my son and me. Henry III still grouses to Henry IV when he visits, complaining about the pain of rejection he has endured for the twenty years that the bird never imprinted on him.

Three of my Henrys have sadly flown from home, the three with no wings. Nowadays, when I call out, "Henry," only one head points toward me, but she is filled with so much compassion, fun, and understanding of the real me, I'm amazed at my great good fortune.

Chapter 13
Peculiar Confidences

Kaethe Kauffman, **At the Museum**, *photo, 2024*

Recently, I have heard three doozies from people who confided in me. I have always delighted in asking folks questions. Could I help it if they answered me?

Real Life—Real Laughs

Giving tours at a local art museum one day, a middle-aged woman named Lana was my sole customer. She loved art and dressed like an abstract painting in a black and white sheath with interlocking rectangular designs. Her umbrella completed the look with contrasting monochrome triangles. For part of the tour, we ventured into the surrounding misty historical gardens. She seemed thrilled by the art, so buoyant, I would not have been surprised if the umbrella lifted her into the air. As she fumbled with her phone, she excitedly explained to me while she dialed that she wanted her husband to join her, to share the joy with him.

I heard his loud voice sputtering with annoyance at the $25 Uber ride he would need, as he declined. Her body sagged, but as we relished more art, her vibrancy returned. Near the end of the tour, she turned to me and blurted, out of the blue, "I've had two affairs."

"Huh?" I replied.

"Yes, two. The first one…" She proceeded to outline the details. Once she became intimate with the fellow, she demanded terms: $5000 per month and a leased car. Her story made me wonder why I had never thought to request a salary and a car from any of my boyfriends in the past. Lana's first affair lasted about six months, complete with salary and car. When he moved away, they had an amicable break-up.

The second man settled with her for $4000 per month and a car. However, he became too demanding, she explained, not allowing her to spend time with her girlfriends.

As a faithful former wife, I choked on indignation while, at the same time, I found myself titillated by her adventurous and entrepreneurial spirit. I wanted to hear more. But my polite docent role forbade me from exclaiming that Lover #2 might have had a point. Paying $4000 a month for her favors might mean he expected priority over her girlfriends. And what about lying to her husband? How could she manage the daily juggling and explain away a new car? In reality, my responses consisted of, "Oh" and "Really?" and "Good Lord."

Like a waitress in a restaurant, I stifled personal opinions to be a good representative of my company, the museum. Perhaps my neutrality fed her need to vent with a seemingly non-judgmental person.

Several days later at the museum another woman, an artist, asked me for a tour of the art show. She wanted photos of herself with paintings and sculptures for her Instagram account. Happy to help, I merrily traipsed through the exhibit with her, laughing while she posed.

Sadly, this museum property, a historical home with manicured acreage, was for sale on the real estate market for $23 million. At the end of the tour, the woman unexpectedly told me her father was a billionaire. My eyes popped. In my experience, Americans were more private about their finances than their sex lives. "Twenty-three million would be chump-change for him," she remarked. "But he's already so busy with other projects, I'll have to persuade him to buy it." She frowned, as if concentrating on which arguments had the best chance.

"Wow," I said, stunned, "that would be great. I'll give him a tour if he wants to look it over." I haven't heard from her yet.

A few days ago, I saw an acquaintance, Matilda, in a drawing class. During a break, she took me aside and furtively told me that she had recently become a countess, a title inherited from an Italian grandfather. Matilda apparently didn't want anyone to overhear, and she swore me to secrecy. Although her family had been in America for several generations, this distinction had recently landed in her lap.

She had always seemed like a serious and honest person, so I didn't doubt her and burst out, "Do you have a castle?"

"Luckily, no," she said. "Can you imagine the upkeep and taxes? But there are lands and art."

And overthrow plots. She somberly reported that, at her grandfather's funeral, all her siblings and cousins demanded she stand down because of being gay. Everyone wanted her younger straight sister to inherit. It sounded horrifyingly medieval. But Matilda held firm, telling them, "As the eldest, I am and will remain the head of this family." I clapped for her.

I asked why she whispered to me, as if the other students would care. She said she had told no one, except her wife. She feared that people's attitudes toward her would change. Others might become deferential, or they might ridicule her. Apparently, being on the cultural frontier as a married homosexual provided enough limelight in her life. But she explained a new phenomenon: many European aristocrats today hid their status, to avoid scammers, false adulation and scorn. I guess some people still have an "off with their heads" attitude toward the privileged. However, Matilda needed to work, so it seemed that an income did not accompany the title.

But why tell me? I had no idea. I had not asked any leading questions. It never occurred to me to inquire about someone's secret aristocratic title.

These three unsolicited revelations shocked me and caught me delightfully unaware each time. But, upon reflection, I admitted to myself that when I first met someone, after I had established an initial rapport, I felt free to ask questions about their children, parents, and where they lived. Maybe they intuitively knew how much I would savor their delectable details.

Chapter 14
Ultra U

How many more fairy tales do I need to come true in my life? I passed almost all the Fairy Tale classes, levels 100 through 400. The difficult courses had provided me with considerable pride of achievement. However, I failed the *Cinderella* course several times. Without it, I couldn't graduate with a Bachelor of Arts degree from the esteemed ULTRA University.

The United League of Traumatizing Renegade Actors, as fairy tale characters prefer to be called, formed an online university, ULTRA U, to better serve a contemporary clientele. Students took fairy tale classes to learn the lesson a particular ULTRA character had to teach. In *The Boy Who Cried Wolf* class, I learned the hazards of lying. The final exam challenged me with a tricky discernment of subtle white lies. I delighted in the "actor," Al, a handsome boyfriend who spoiled me with a secure lifestyle in a high-end neighborhood. This class took me fifteen years to complete; the final exam included my discovery of his secret love affairs which had involved years of lies. Although I had to apply for several extensions, I passed the class because Al provided 4,672 lies for me to discover, a difficult curriculum for a trusting gal like me. I am proud that I discovered 4,532 of them, giving me an "A."

In the *Hansel and Gretel* class, I learned to detect essential evil in a person, even if they sported an outer façade that looked to be delicious as candy and cookies. In each class, we navigated and resolved real-life situations. Some men I had dated had delectable and especially edible exteriors, hiding an inner sociopath. There were more of these than I could have imagined, including: Sven, the lovely art model who stole cars; Bill, the ruddy Outward Bound instructor who hid a gambling addiction; and the tall Olaf, an irresistible attorney who dealt drugs on the side. I wrote such good term papers on these three, I aced the class.

The *Little Red Riding Hood* course refined my acumen for evil lurking in a sweet guise, such as a poor bed-ridden grandmother. Everyone loved Brad, the compassionate male nurse who seemed to adore his dying patients. Eventually people noticed that people did not live long in his care, although no one ever proved he hastened their deaths.

Thanks to my superb ULTRA teachers, I have learned to see disguises and to run away, when necessary, like the handsome humorous guy I dated who pretended to be a doctor. It only took me three weeks to learn the truth; he was a paper-pusher for a health organization. When I broke up with Brad and, later, with Mr. Non-Doctor, I'm proud to announce, I passed *Little Red Riding Hood* 201 and 301.

The *Persephone* series of classes taught me how to behave in hell and how to get out. The Greek goddess, Persephone, had been raped by Hades and dragged into the underworld. Although she suffered in a literal hell, Persephone had the wits to work out a deal with him. She lived in the underworld half the year, counseling the shocked and anguished newly arrived souls. Her time there became winter above ground because her mother, Demeter, goddess of the Earth, grieved so much that all life stopped growing. When Persephone emerged into the upper world, spring and summer blossomed, much to Demeter's ecstasy.

My next-door neighbor, Howard, daily proclaimed how hard he worked in his home office, when I knew from his wife he lived on an inheritance and spent his days on porn sites. His ongoing obsessive deceptions kept him in Persephone's underworld. He didn't know his wife confided in me. I quietly observed the huge energies he invested in reporting to me and other neighbors how tough his daily stock market research was, how time-

Real Life—Real Laughs

consuming his conference calls, how draining his extensive financial reports. While I nodded and commiserated, I noticed that, over the months and years, I did not become tempted to gossip to others about the false front of his hidden life. This constituted a big achievement for me who loved long "tell-all" sessions with friends and neighbors. I recognized Howard's self-imposed ego-trap, a meaningless and anxious underworld for him and hell for his family. Although I couldn't imagine how the family held together, I learned not to judge them. In this way, I passed the *Persephone* 101 test.

Being a natural blabbermouth, I felt fortunate to also value the exhilaration of silence at times. After all, Persephone lived in the underworld of secrets half the year and emerged into the upper world of honesty for the other half. When I created a new painting or wrote a story, I kept quiet and savored it as uniquely mine. I had always believed secrets were delusional; people around the secret-keeper picked up the tension of hidden agendas, if not the details. But I savored my fleeting secrets, delicious whether in paint or written words.

As I learned in *Persephone* 201, concealments needed to eventually evolve from a tender and private place into a public venue. Every six months, Persephone came back to the earth's surface and brought spring, new life. When my current delectable project became unbearable, a natural gestation period ended with the overwhelming need to push the hidden creation out into the world. Sooner or later, I showed my new painting to others or read the story to my writing group. These events flowed into the common consciousness where they had the chance to be amended by society's opinions and ethics. If my work had broken a moral code, I would have become mortified and changed. By letting secrets soar, they freed themselves from Persephone's hell and I finished *Persephone* 201.

More horrible was the cousin who had a breast cancer scare. I watched her husband do everything in his power to keep her from going to the doctor for further tests: car "breakdowns," temper tantrums about how stupid she was to trust her doctors, and refusals to pay medical bills. His behavior seemed so bizarre; I came to suspect he possibly planned a divorce but hadn't told his wife yet. He seemed overjoyed that nature had potentially handed him a better alternative to his third divorce. I ached for her as we traversed and unraveled each step in her discovery process: the car was fine, her doctors trustable, she and I together had enough money to pay for the biopsy. I held her hand as she did so. Luckily, my cousin's diagnosis proved to be negative for cancer and positive for divorce within the year. This type of soap opera, an exciting hell, appealed to me in my younger years, but not since I passed *Persephone* 301.

The *Persephone* series had one more level, a tough final term. One sunny fall afternoon I unsuspectingly went to my doctor for a routine visit, light-hearted. One half-hour later, I staggered out of her office, deep in Persephone's winter, for tests had shown I had cancer, and it had already spread. The doctor cried with me. For the next year, I trudged through all the hellish cures society offered with the best of intentions: cut, poison and burn.

Wounded, but grateful for each remedy, I tried to apply the lessons from *Persephone* 101, 201 and 301. But now I was not safely observing my neighbor or cousin. I found myself in modern medicine's trenches and felt the assault on my body and mind. Yet, somehow, I remained willing to plod through each step, bit by bit on the path through hell.

I learned a fresh perspective on the ancient Buddhist philosophy of impermanence. Change remained certain. As one friend observed, "The treatments will end within a year, and either you will be cured or dead. But at least, they will be over."

I brightened at this news. On this horrible path, reaching the end became the most important goal, no matter whether the changes meant health or a metamorphosis into noble worm metabolism, the great earth recyclers. Both looked equally okay in the middle of what seemed like never-ending surgeries, radiation and chemotherapy. But I persevered, day by day, passed *Persephone* 401 and, so far, have lived to write the story.

My failure with the *Cinderella* class remained a considerable blot on my academic record. Prior to my work with Persephone, I had been stuck concerning phony female power: attractiveness or the lack of it. I wanted to be Cinderella, to have a man discover my true hidden beauty, which equaled love, in my naïve view. But why did we leave this critical task up to a young male, the prince, who, if under 25, still had an unformed cerebral cortex? And if over 25, he had tender new critical thinking skills he hadn't learned how to fully use. I suspect this is why I flunked the course: I still wanted the prince, no matter how mentally impaired. Accordingly, before I had finished the *Persephone* courses, ULTRA U provided various men to test how much I craved male appreciation at any price.

With Hiram, at sixty, an interesting and talented man close to my age, I made a seemingly safe assumption that he had mature frontal lobes. After a few evenings of fascinating philosophical discussions, Hiram confided in me that he heard voices in his head.

"Pleasant ones, I hope," I said.

"No, bad ones, but medication keeps their volume low," Hiram explained.

"How nice," I responded, instantly aware of the red message that my desperation meter flashed at me.

"Don't go there," the messages repeated. I listened, even though I felt sorry for this sympathetic, but mentally injured man.

For a few months, I dated a kind, generous fellow who, I eventually realized, had consistently found reasons not to introduce me to his friends and family. He swore devoted monogamy to me, but, in the third month, I found out he had a girlfriend hidden away. I tried to feel good that it only took me three months to find out, not a bad statistic considering a possible 90-year life span.

In those pre-*Persephone* class days, I had been Cinderella enough to desire to transform my metaphorical rags (old face) into a ball gown (young face). I visited my local spa for an analysis. But everything they recommended would hurt: Botox shots, laser zaps to the face, and exfoliation. I was a spa wimp.

After I had finished *Persephone* 401, post-cancer, the *Cinderella* courses lost their allure. I felt so happy to feel the life force coursing through my veins, it seemed that cancer had brought a better Prince Charming to me: my inner self with an essence of exuberance within. As life proceeded, good friends and lovers came and went, but the ups and downs did not sway my essential joy in life.

I sent a letter to ULTRA U saying I had ditched the Cinderella story. It had lost its relevance in my life. I assumed this disqualified me from their program. After so many years of work and getting close to the end, I grieved, but decided to be true to myself.

To my surprise, they mailed my degree with a letter saying,

Dear Ms. Burns,

We support your *Cinderella* course rejection. Some people need to live out the story, others don't. Your insight into Cinderella's irrelevance to your life is a victory.

We enclose your official ULTRA University Bachelor of Arts degree along with all the considerable benefits and privileges it confers upon you. Congratulations.

Sincerely,

Dr. Rumpelstiltskin (no relation to the ancient infamous historical figure)

ULTRA University President

Chapter 15
The Older Woman

Kaethe Kauffman, **Older Woman**, *oil, graphite, 12"x9", 2024*

Real Life—Real Laughs

Whenever I visited my artist friend Josie in New York, I knew something remarkable would happen. It always did. Last month, when we had finished viewing an art exhibit close to High Line Park in West Chelsea, she asked if I wanted to drop in on a nearby friend.

"Sure," I replied.

While we walked along the old rail track toward her friend Lisbeth's apartment, Josie told me her buddy was well known in the music world for her antique violas and occasionally played as a guest with the New York Philharmonic.

"Wow," I said, impressed.

After we had knocked on Lisbeth's door, Josie suddenly said, "Oh, just so you know, Lisbeth is ninety years old." Before I could digest this, the door swung open to reveal a woman who looked to be in her sixties, strong and vibrant with a welcoming smile.

After an effusive greeting, Lisbeth gushed that her boyfriend had just left a birthday gift for her, a portrait of them together. I imagined an old guy with a walker. She lifted a lovely photo, framed in hand-painted and rough-hewn wood, of her and a black-haired man with lovely smooth skin, certainly not a nonagenarian. When I peered more closely, I detected subtle grey at his temples.

"Well, he's a cutie," I said.

She quickly cued me in, "Randy is fifty-five years old and I met him online. He prefers older women," she bluntly said.

My mouth dropped open in shock. I had heard of cougars, women ten to fifteen years older than partners, but Lisbeth was the first lady I'd met who was 35 years older than her mate. I hoped she represented a trend.

Since she wasn't shy about her boyfriend, I asked, "What kind of profile did you post?"

"Oh, I lied," she cheerfully said. "I was 85 at the time, but who's going to date an 85-year-old? So, I said I was 80." Josie and I chuckled.

"Hey, check out her violas," Josie said, leading us to one end of the living room where two instruments caught the afternoon sun where they rested upright on wooden pedestals. We oohed and aahed over the exquisite violas in rich dark walnut colors that resembled scrumptious chocolate. Their sounds would have probably melted my heart.

I could not resist asking more questions about Lisbeth's personal life. "Did Randy ever find out you lied?" I asked.

"Oh, yes, as I got close to 90, I figured I should come clean. By then, Randy had proven his devotion. He's the real deal. His last girlfriend had been 85 when she died. When I told him my real age, he acted like I had given him the best gift ever. He got excited, really happy that I was older than he had thought." Lisbeth grinned at the memory.

I shook my head, astounded that such a man existed. I couldn't let it go. "But, do you have kids?"

"Oh, yeah, we both do. Our children think we're weird. My son says Randy's a gold digger." Lisbeth giggled, "But there's no gold." I looked around at her cozy, modest apartment that held nothing of much value except the two violas, and neither was a Stradivarius.

"Sounds like a love match. Good for you," I said.

"He's younger than my son and daughter and they'll probably never like him," she continued with a resigned, but slightly impish shrug of one shoulder.

I nodded, unable to imagine dating someone younger than my 26-year-old son. I beamed at her in admiration. Up close, I could see her facial skin had become mottled with age, bumpy like old snow. From a few feet away, I didn't notice it.

"You're an inspiration," I told her.

I thought about my six aunts as they had aged. In the 1950s, middle-class women "got old": their faces wrinkled, and they tinted their white hair with a purple rinse to balance the natural yellowish hue of age. But the lavender looked worse, a badge that said, "old woman." In their seventies, their bosoms fell to their waists, and they wore dresses with miniature realistic floral prints. My black and white photographs of them preserved this quaint, now historic phenomenon.

My aunts were homesteading pioneers who later enjoyed the roaring twenties, survived the depression, and traveled the globe as nurses in World War II. They had kicked up their heels, worn Vogue fashions (hand-sewn, but from Vogue patterns), had illegitimate and legitimate babies, my cousins and me; smart ladies, as adventurous and rebellious as the women of my 1960s generation, albeit without reliable birth control.

But they aged in the traditional ways, no longer socially acceptable. Today, Victoria's Secret keeps our breasts high. Fifty brands of hair colors disguise our grays and whites. Facial laser treatments mean we don't have to get expensive facelifts to chase wrinkles away. The "old woman" tiny-realistic-flowered dress has disappeared. Now everyone, even 90-year-olds like Lisbeth, wears fashionable styles, including skin-tight spandex, trendy and good-looking.

Lisbeth appeared healthy and happy, and I cheered her on. She opened me to a new vision. "Hurray for Lisbeth," I told Josie as we left her apartment. "She's fabulous."

Chapter 16
Smart Water

Kaethe Kauffman and James Haydn Kauffman Hite, **Smart Water**, *collage from photos, 2024*

Water has intelligence. As novelist Tom Robbins explained in *Even Cowgirls Get the Blues*, water originally designed humans, composed of 65% H2O, as receptacles to carry it world-wide. Mankind experienced a recent pandemic, spread by droplets of fluid that reached across the globe like a viral tsunami. Daily, people of every age and race prove their efficiency as pathogen wet nurses, making Robbins' theory plausible. Water as a clever god has ancient roots.

Honored by the early Greeks, Gaia, our primal mother Earth with all her fresh waters, and Poseidon, god of the seas, ruled over people. The Greeks understood their correct position in relationship to omnipotent nature.

Even in our secular modern era, we acknowledge water's power. In the *Star Trek, The Next Generation* television series, aliens communicated with Captain Pickard using their label for humans, "Ugly Bags of Water," a name Commander Data pointed out is technically accurate.

Dr. Masau Emoto, a Japanese researcher, found that water reacts to human consciousness. In response to beautiful words, music or pictures, water forms harmonic, exquisite crystals. After exposure to pollution or hard rock noise, misshapen blobs emerge when frozen.

With their large brains, humans claim to be at the top of the food chain, to be the smartest creatures on earth, as evaluated by themselves. And yet a brainless virus apparently signed a transportation contract with water and brought our entire social order to its knees, killing about fifteen million people.

The virus piggybacked on us as we traveled on our extensive networks via airplanes, trains, cars, and buses. It congregated with us in convention centers, stadiums, schools, and office buildings. Prior to the pandemic, we felt safe on public transport and in large buildings, smug in our dominion over nature, traveling faster in vehicles than we could run, or sitting in a climate-controlled room. We usually limited our fear to a nutty member of our own species who might suddenly attack. In public places, as we spewed droplets on each other, the virus found heaven in the watery medium between us which linked millions of humans around the world. Hitchhiking on invisible splatter, Covid-19 found new hosts and replicated to an unimaginable degree.

Who is the smart one now? Perhaps we should sign a peace treaty with Gaia and Poseidon. Or we might form a new contemporary spiritual belief in hydro-theology, a word my sister, a water engineer, uses to describe her personal relationship with her beloved life study. If we humbly acknowledge our dependency on the great liquefied realm around us and concede its superiority, perhaps we can come into alignment with nature's reality. Her forces are smarter than us and infinitely more powerful. Maybe playing sweet music to all the water on earth might engender the gods' sympathy for weak humanity. Perhaps Gaia, Poseidon, or the hydro-theology spirits won't sign the next virus contract that comes across their desk.

Chapter 17
I Thought I Was Interesting

Kaethe Kauffman, **Astounded**, *oil paint on photo, 12x10, 2020*

When I realize someone doesn't like me, I suffer a rude awakening. I pride myself on getting along with people. However, a few examples to the contrary come to mind.

For the last 18 years, a woman at work, Sue, has been repeatedly paired with me on major projects. I thought she would see that I am a hard worker and enthusiastic about our tasks. Naturally, she would like me.

But Sue had one goal in life: to spot famous people and find a way to talk to them and report back to everyone. Our work, organizing tours at a local museum, rarely provided access to the stellar rock musicians she coveted. I seldom recognized their names and so could not join in her enthusiasm. She quickly perceived my lack of interest when I ran out of responses after I had said, "Great," "Nice," and "Good luck." She began to avoid me. When work threw us together, she looked the other way, treating me with disdain, as if I were pitiful for not venerating Tom Paxton, Robbie Robertson or John Cale. She had met someone of that caliber on a golf course and gushed endlessly over him.

As the years went on, she mostly ignored me. Although I discussed our kids, who were the same age, and the latest gossip at work, she seemed to have put me in a box: boring. In the last few years, I accepted we would never be buddies.

For 20 years, I belonged to a civic volunteer group. Ten years ago, a new woman joined. Her husband, Jacob, came to our occasional picnics, bringing his homemade cookies which I always praised. He rarely spoke to me but responded with a slight grin when I thanked him for his latest baked goods. I considered him shy.

But last year, he startled me when he walked across the lawn and hailed me with a stream of questions. I had never heard him talk so much. In the past six months, due to Covid cancellations and re-scheduling and other mistakes, I had gone on two big trips, back-to-back: one to Southeast Asia and one to Turkey with my son. I couldn't resist posting photos on Facebook of me on a camel and in front of Vietnamese Buddhist statues. This seemed to excite Jacob, and he wanted to know about my travels. Did I intend to go on more trips, perhaps around the world?

As we chatted, I found myself bemused by this new side of Jacob, who had been quiet around me for ten years. It seemed he wasn't an introvert but had previously found me uninteresting. I laughed at myself. I preferred to imagine him tongue-tied rather than suppose he thought I was dull. He seemed disappointed that I had no grand scheme to traverse the globe. He might not speak to me again for another decade. With Sue and Jacob, I felt surprised at my misjudgment, but not hurt. We had not been friends.

However, with Rebecca, a sharp pain pierced my chest when I discovered she didn't reciprocate the friendship I thought we enjoyed. For thirteen years, our children attended the same schools and sports teams. In the child-raising trenches, we shared room-mother tasks and endlessly discussed our kids' highs and lows. We formed a folk music group with a couple of others and performed old Pete Seeger and Woody Guthrie songs occasionally. When I discovered I needed to separate from my partner of thirty years, she was the first person I told. In recent years, our music group had not performed much, but we got together to practice every two weeks or so.

Last year, in a group conversation, a recent friend thanked Rebecca for the wonderful retirement party Rebecca had thrown for herself the week before. I felt astonished that I was not invited. What a shocking and humbling moment.

I believe the old adage that humility is good for the soul. Awkward situations can prompt insights. I have accepted I can't always have a friendship with some people, no matter how hard I try. However, I still prefer to assume I'm an interesting person.

Chapter 18
A Good Boy

Last December I asked my little neighbor, Toby, a typical adult question, "Do you think Santa's coming this year?" Solemn, he silently nodded. I squatted next to Toby as he sat in his mom's jogging stroller on the sidewalk.

I only saw him every few months and we didn't know each other well. To pass the slightly awkward time until his mom returned from grabbing something she had forgotten inside her house, I asked another thoughtless question. "Have you been a good boy?"

A frown creased his face as he seemed to struggle with an internal debate, fingers fluttering in the air. "Well, I think so." He looked this way and that, as if he were worried about the bad things he had done.

I felt terrible. He seemed to have taken my flippant query seriously and struggled in an existential debate about good and evil.

I tried to sugarcoat it, "I'll bet you're a good boy most of the time."

He looked doubtful and thought for a moment, then his eyebrows shot up with apparent enlightenment. "Yeah,

I'm being a good boy right now." He smiled, seeming happy to make a positive report of himself.

"Yes, you are," I said, relieved that he placidly sat in his stroller and didn't fuss in his mom's absence.

This thought faded for a moment because, all at once, a memory of an ex-boyfriend flashed to mind. He had said the same thing as Toby when I discovered his years of cheating on me. The boyfriend had explained, with anger, "None of this mattered until you found out." In his case, *appearing* to be a good boy was apparently all that counted. He quickly became a footnote in my life story.

Maybe society's Santa Claus myth prompted our children to have an early acquaintance with good and evil, providing a way for a young conscience to develop.

But I hoped Toby would not evolve into a person who did the right thing only when Santa's reckoning, or a wronged girlfriend's judgment, loomed large. Toby, at least, seemed to tussle with his conscience, a good sign of future maturity.

Chapter 19
Busy Birds

Among birds, it apparently matters who you spend the night with. At sunset, I love to wander outdoors to hear the raucous and high-pitched chirping and squawking from the tops of trees. The intense sounds make me laugh. I take great comfort in the birds' busy squabbling. Animal research has found that birds' sounds lower human blood pressure and release endorphins, soothing us. At our primal core, our instincts register that birds' ongoing communication with each other means that no predators are around to hear the songsters' locations. A silent forest is a dangerous one. The evening avian cacophony seems to pump a boatload of happy body chemistry throughout my system.

As the sun dips low, what do the little feathered beings get riled up about? Google tells me the male birds, seeking dominant territory on a branch and the best mate, make most of the noise. After a day of searching for worms and insects, those birds with the fullest tummies have the energy to fight for the safest place to sleep and the most desirable mate. I imagine the strongest males bunking down on the widest, most stable part of a branch, near the trunk. Then I realize that the tree's trunk could be a superhighway for snakes or rats. However, the tips of the branches are narrow and might wildly swing in gusts of wind. From a bird's perspective, there must be dozens of other safety factors I can't imagine.

Likewise, with mate selection, I don't know if prospective bird paramours find each other via attractive pheromones or feather color or ways I can't perceive. I only know that it involves complicated and loud communications at sunset. When camping under big trees, I have noticed the same phenomenon at sunrise. Perhaps birds reevaluate anew who to spend the day with each morning.

Upon reflection, I wonder if human territory establishment and mate selection are just as loud and complicated as the birds. People, like our winged friends, spend enormous amounts of time and energy searching for the best home. The ultimate in human territory conflict is warfare, a noisy business indeed.

The human quest for a perfect partner may be as complicated as it seems to be with birds. Courting rituals, Valentine's Day, social media, the garment and cosmetic industries, and advertising all show us how to appear sexy and find a mate. As for noise, at a recent BTS concert in a Las Vegas stadium, 50,000 screaming fans idolized the heavily made-up, wildly gesticulating and loud young males onstage. Birds resemble humans more than I thought.

Part Three

Keeping Sane, Mostly

Kaethe Kauffman, **Rollers**, *oil, graphite, 11"x8", 2020*

Chapter 20
Odd Hairdressers

Why is it hard to find a good hairdresser? I want a simple "bob" haircut (longer on the sides than the layered back), which I would think is standard. But apparently it is not. When I meet a new stylist and make my request for a "bob," most hem and haw and turn me over to someone who reluctantly takes a stab at my head, usually with peculiar results.

Throughout the 1960s, 70s, 80s, and 90s, my mother went for her weekly "hair therapy," as she called it. I never met her hairstylist, but each Saturday, Mom returned home with fresh peroxide, a hardened bouffant shell around her head and a happy mood. Naturally, I grew up expecting that, as an adult, I could depend on regular sessions at a hair salon to cheer me up.

However, when venturing out to a new salon, I quake as I remember strange past experiences.

Recommended by a friend whose fashionable hair I admired, I visited Hank. He gives his clients fifteen minutes of cutting and monologues about his latest vacation video editing efforts. He charges $100 for the quarter hour which would have been okay if my hair didn't look like chopped spinach when he had finished.

Another friend raved about Francois. After another $100, my hair looked exactly the same. Only several tiny wisps were cut, even after I made repeated requests for the "bob" which would have required a major remodel on the back of my head.

One day, when wandering around a mall, I bravely entered a new salon and met Candy, who looked nothing like her name. She was a kindly but scrawny older woman with shorn gray hair that sat like a swimming cap atop her head. She dawdled over me with tiny scissors for an hour or more. I lost track of time. When I looked in the mirror, I saw the desired bob style, glory hallelujah! When I asked if she would trim a little more in a couple of spots, she happily obliged. I had found my stylist. Over the next year, I noticed each visit got longer, until it lasted more than ninety minutes. When I suggested she use a razor on my neck to speed things along, she sounded shocked. "Oh, I couldn't do that. I don't use razors, only scissors." This struck me as unnecessarily time-consuming, but I am usually relaxed and didn't mind.

At the next appointment, I told Candy I had to leave in forty-five minutes for a doctor's appointment. She went into a tailspin. Her hands shook. "I can't do this," she said. Then she confessed that she has severe OCD, obsessive compulsive disorder. She awakens at 4am every morning so she can accomplish her numerous rituals before she comes to work at 10am. I was shocked. I learned more about OCD, a progressive disease that caused Candy to create ever more rituals, prolonging her haircuts. I now realized what a strain it would be for her to cut my hair in any time under ninety minutes. A few months later, I got a new demanding job and could no longer indulge in the increasing time Candy needed to cut every hair with her small scissors.

Eventually, I tried Great Clips, a $15 hair salon in my neighborhood. There I met my next stylist, Kim, who turned out to be a countess. She had just returned from vacation, two weeks at a Renaissance fair where she was a lady in waiting in the court of the queen. Having participated in these fairs for over two decades, she proudly explained that she started as a handmaiden and worked her way up to her current high status. How interesting that becoming an aristocrat can be based on meritocracy. Only in America.

I asked Lady Kim many questions about being a countess. It seemed real to her. Regardless, she produced an elegant "bob," and I adore her. I'll address her with any title she wants for such a beautiful haircut. I hope I have found my forever hairdresser. But she is so dedicated to her Renaissance world, I worry she might get promoted there. Queen Kim may not deign to cut hair any longer.

Chapter 21
Pandemic Itch

Kaethe Kauffman, **Pandemic Nose**, *oil, graphite, 14"x11", 2020*

    Until the pandemic mandate to avoid touching our faces, I thought I rarely laid a finger on that piece of anatomy other than to apply my daily face cream. In accord with a universal truism, the minute something became forbidden, I had to do it. My head seemed to erupt in hundreds of itches all day. Scientific studies claimed the average to be sixteen to twenty-three times per hour. Humans seemed to be the only animals who did this. I theorized that viruses have taken over. Our skin has become more agitated because Covid19 stuck its tiny crowns onto our smooth surfaces and demanded we soothe the spots. Innocently, we scratched and, with infected fingers, unknowingly spread the disease. What a cunning little virus.

When I first observed the places on my face that demanded an immediate scratch, I thought, *this will be an easy case of mind over matter. I'll relax, do a mini-meditation and tell the irritation to go away.* Positive thinking worked on minor feathery agitations, but others shocked me with their virulence. They felt deep and insistent, as if rubbing the area raw might not quell the itch.

I began to seriously explore why certain fleeting facial aggravations became compelling. The nose proved to be the hot spot. Why? Perhaps my nostrils were extra sensitive, like dogs, although I had never observed my former dogs scratching their noses. Probably the smart virus targeted a germy part of my countenance for tickle attacks with its usual expansion motives in mind.

Breaking down likely occurrences by time of day helped me to cope. I had no desire to paw at my face in the mornings. Perhaps, by afternoon, my visage had tired from the day's work and begged for rest and comfort. *Just take a moment and spoil me with a tender ministration*, my nose seemed to say. *And if you don't, I'll force you.* To prove my theory, the prickly parts became worse in the late afternoon and evening when a major itch storm might hit at any moment. With no obvious cause, it felt like a tiny hair waved in a one-centimeter circle near my left nostril. My willpower yelling, *Don't touch it!* proved worthless.

For months, I waged this battle, determined to control these skin tingles with my mind. Every day I lost, scratched my face and washed my hands. At last, three and one-half months into the Covid19 era, I gave up on mind control. A simple solution occurred to me. In the afternoons and evenings, I carried a facial tissue at all times to wipe a suddenly distressed area, thus sparing my fingers contamination.

Two months later, I began drawing self-portraits, experimenting with different art styles from realistic to abstract. But one drawing, against my conscious will, developed an enormous and elaborate nose. I inherited my mother's beaky English snout with a knot in the middle, but it wasn't nearly as large and uneven as the one I drew.

Tempted to destroy the obnoxious drawing, something compelled me to keep looking at it day after day.

All at once, I understood. This giant nose demonstrated how my proboscis felt in the late afternoons and evenings. It seemed like it had become bait and ballooned larger, attracting itches. With Kleenex in hand, I laughed at the drawing, which no longer appeared so dreadful.

Chapter 22
Introvert Heaven

Kaethe Kauffman**, Introvert Heaven**, *watercolor, 10"x9", 2016*

Real Life—Real Laughs

Aside from the threat of imminent, hideous death by asphyxiation, I have never felt so supremely happy as during the pandemic. As an introvert, I had always suffered as a person who craved quiet in a noisy world. Cities assumed everyone wanted a stadium or a convention center. With successful bond-raising efforts and, once built, maintaining a full schedule, it appeared people loved to gather. Baffled, all I could do was shake my head and stay away. My adult son couldn't believe I had never attended a rock concert. "You could've seen the greats in their prime, the Eagles, Led Zeppelin, Pink Floyd," he said, confounded.

"But the concerts were crowded and noisy," I replied, even though I knew this made no sense to him. But I would sooner face Hell than a rock concert.

I have always wondered why society considered solitary confinement a punishment. If I had been an exceptionally good prisoner, I could imagine the matron rewarding me, "Cate, you've earned the highest honor we bestow, a month all by yourself." How I would beam with joy and relish the stillness.

Now, during the pandemic, society sent me comforting messages: stay inside, keep six feet away from others and never gather with more than ten people, isolate, don't go to the office. They described a homebody's heaven.

Real Life—Real Laughs

All my life, I forced myself to socialize because I should enjoy it, according to friends, family, therapists, and self-help books. I attended temple, performed jobs with groups of people, gave volunteer tours at museums. Suddenly, our mayor and governor told us to do the opposite. I shed a heavy burden I had carried for a lifetime.

My pandemic world was a wonder. For the first time, I could be exactly who I had always been on the inner level. When I canceled all my meetings, I demonstrated good citizenship, a complete amazement to me. I skipped around my condo, humming to myself. When I wore myself out, I meditated for as long as I wanted. I worked in solitude in my art studio, happy as could be. I called a friend or family member every few days, when it suited me. I took long walks, staying away from others. As required by my city, I wore a face mask and felt more relaxed. I didn't have to wear lipstick or make-up, those fussy societal requirements for females. I understood how Middle Eastern women's face coverings might be nice for them.

For the first time in my life, I can be who I truly am, an out-of-the-closet loner. I openly love my solitude and feel appreciated by my culture for adhering to those standards. I had not realized how much society's approval meant to me.

I feel bad that I have been enjoying this time while others suffer. Apparently, possible death is the only force that can make solitary behaviors become the norm in society. At least, if I get sick and it is my time to go, I'll die happy, a fulfilled introvert.

Chapter 23
Pleased Protoplasm

Kaethe Kauffman, **Pleased Protoplasm**, *ink, collage, 16"x16", 2022*

I did not plan to become a blob and I certainly did not imagine I would enjoy the experience. Like much of my life, it happened accidentally.

Real Life—Real Laughs

I literally sailed off the grid into remote Alaska and Canada to relish hiking and kayaking. I spotted whales, grizzlies, orcas, and eagles daily, happily absorbing more wilderness than I had been able to do in the past several years of Covid restrictions.

On the seventh day of the trip on a small ship with 39 passengers, I assumed I had a bad reaction to a new seasickness medicine, a slightly itchy throat and low energy. The next day, after a long walk on land to hopefully chase the meds out of my system, I felt worse with lower energy, a sore throat and headache. I admitted to myself I had come down with a cold. A Covid test from the ship's doctor proved to be negative, as I knew it would. In the midst of all this fresh air, how could a Covid germ survive? I settled down to a day of rest, which, being out of cell phone and internet range, meant reading and writing. Keeping the headache away with Tylenol, I thoroughly enjoyed a quiet time, knowing I would feel better the next day.

However, when morning came, the world felt very different. I simply lay still on my cabin bunk. I did not think or plan or analyze, all my favorite mental activities. I experienced perfect contentment being stationary. I quelled the increasing headache with Tylenol, laid back, and let myself be a piece of protoplasm. I felt good and complete, a happy blob. Seven hours passed in this peaceful and idyllic, yet wide-awake, state. Later, it occurred to me that Buddhist monks might call this experience one of "emptiness" or "void," free of all ego and attachment to phenomena. At the time, I loved it and never wanted it to end.

By one in the afternoon, I finally realized that lovely as it was, being a drifting piece of joy constituted a highly abnormal situation. Yesterday, I had spent my time mentally stimulated, reading and writing. A day later, I lacked the mental or physical desire, and perhaps ability, to do either. However, I felt so good, I hadn't considered a negative interpretation to my new reality. Now I remembered another symptom people commonly mentioned with Covid: exhaustion. That's when I knew I needed another Covid test. This one proved I had the disease.

Deep inside, I recognized the truth of my diagnosis. Without Tylenol, I had a killer headache and a throat on fire. I accepted my Covid as real and appreciatively took the anti-viral medicine offered. By now, many of my friends had had Covid, so I didn't feel alone. The ship's rules kept me in a five-day quarantine, but the crew spoiled me with gourmet meals, daily health care, stimulating scientific lectures piped into my room, the world's most beautiful scenery floating by my large window, walks outside when the rest of the passengers had disembarked at a port. I couldn't remember a time when I had been so spoiled.

Luckily, I healed within the usual couple of weeks once I got home. I felt extremely grateful to have avoided the disease in its earlier, more lethal forms.

However, I remembered those unusually serene seven hours I had spent before the positive Covid test. As pleasant as it was, in reality, my inactivity in a tranquil world may have provided more time for the virus to expand. Maybe the sneaky bug excreted knock-out chemicals into my system, rendering me unwilling to fight back. If so, my clever enemy gained seven hours' advantage with its siege on my system.

On the other hand, I had never heard anyone refer to "Covid bliss," so perhaps those hours were unique to me, a gift of calm abiding. I normally meditate each day, so perhaps my mind and body intuitively knew to take advantage of my hours in quarantine. Whatever its source, I treasure the memory of seven hours of pure peace, fully conscious and satisfied basking in simple existence.

Chapter 24
Kelvins Are Forever

James Haydn Kauffman Hite, **Kaethe Kauffman turning the Wheel of Dharma at a Buddhist Theme Park, Thailand**, *photo, 2020*

    A sense of timelessness can be addictive. I love to get lost in a splurge of endorphins which put me in a zone where minutes or hours lack reality, such as the famous runners' high (in my case, a walker's tingly cheer). Other activities that produce joyful time-free awareness are calm meditation, singing an opera aria (badly, but endorphins don't care), painting a masterpiece (the optimistic internal chemistry fooling me into believing I have created a work of art), sex that seems to cement a true bond forever (thank you, hormones), laughter with good friends, and closeness with family that seems as if it might never end. Nature entices me with tastes of the sublime where I seem to float outside the realm of ticking clocks. But no matter how real and endless seeming, each illusory suspension of time provides a fleeting experience. Having been given a small taste, I am left to pine for a prolonged experience of forever.

    For now, all my hints of the eternal seem real during their exquisite small moments, so wonderful that I make them a priority in my life. I create art, sing, exercise, meditate, love my family and friends, hike in nature, relish sex and laughter, attend yoga classes. Adding up all these activities means I spend a lot of time with small pieces of infinity. I aim to increase the amount daily, as if the tiny bits I string together can create a boundless golden chain. Meanwhile, my many peeks at timelessness make existence more fun.

Real Life—Real Laughs

If I look at empirical evidence, for most of my life, experiences started, then stopped. Time existed in chunks; something happened and, sometime later, it ended. In childhood, every March, we bought baby chickens at the feed store to raise in our chicken coop. For weeks, I gushed over the darling little peepers. Over the summer, they quickly grew and became adults. By the fall, the hens terrified me with hard pecks to keep me away from their eggs. Noisy roosters appeared on our dinner plates. Each segment of time progressed forward, bit by bit.

My parents died 40 years apart, but each death felt like the hack of a machete that sliced away an epoch of my life. These segments of time gave me building blocks which I placed in a certain configuration that, all together, equaled a life design which I created, bit by bit.

But oddly, amid my designer blocks, I tripped into a timeless zone that I hadn't expected: marriage. Only true love could have been at play because I had never planned to marry. But, all at once, Mr. Perfect appeared and after four years of fun and adventure, it seemed natural to make our bond permanent. After the joyful ceremony, I felt as though I had unexpectedly made a commitment to his ancestors and to mine. Had I also married great-grandfather Bill Bannister with the giant mutton-chop whiskers? Yes, I had. In my mind, I felt forever linked to this lineage. Had I indulged in an over-romanticized mindset? Perhaps, but I don't remember ever consciously considering such a thing. In fact, my mother's fourteen fiancés and three marriages devalued the institution for me. Nonetheless, upon marriage, I saw myself as part of endless great-grandparents, and I felt honored by my place in the family line. We had a dearly loved son, and we three nobly stood in the timeline of relatedness.

Were there other realms of infinity that I had overlooked? Yes, I hadn't considered the most obvious and yet, oddly abstract.

Our bodies exist as an energetic system. Physicists tell us our energy can never be lost; however, it will drastically change when we die.

Realistically, we all know we will die one day, and our body nutrients will feed worms (if buried) or plants (if cremated). The Tibetans prefer "sky burial," direct transformation into vulture vitality. One way or the other, our vigor conversion takes place, and we retain the same number of Kelvins forever—degrees of energy as measured by physicists. This has been proven many times in the First Law of Thermodynamics. Whether we became weeds or a tiger's lunch (on an unfortunate safari), our energy remains constant. That's the type of infinity I can count on. But I put off taking my personal Kelvins seriously no matter how long I worked for hospice and sympathized with others who looked their pending Kelvin transformations directly in the eye.

My adult son, Jon, found another way to clutch a sense of the eternal in spite of death, one I never imagined. When our alpha 21-year-old cockatiel bird Henry died, my 27-year-old son and I sobbed together. Like a playful, rascally little sibling to Jon, Henry ran our household with her loud chirps, usually demanding head-scratches (hers, not ours) and games. We missed her terribly. Once we found a moment free of tears, Jon said with a shaky voice, "Mom, how should we preserve Henry's DNA?"

"Huh?" I replied, preoccupied by how many plastic bags poor Henry required to avoid freezer burn in her temporary resting place. I also silently questioned whether pet crematoriums were real and, if so, did any exist nearby? I had no idea what Jon's words meant.

"Well, why don't you study that project while I research pet crematoriums?" I asked Jon. But I muttered under my breath, "This is too weird for me." After hard crying gave way to sporadic grieving in a day or two, I realized my techy son needed science to help him feel an eternal connection to the family member he adored for all the years he could remember. Love for Henry bequeathed a sense of infinity to Jon and, strangely, Henry's DNA preservation allowed Jon to express it. However, the details proved to be gruesome: four bloody muscle samples excised by a surprised but willing vet, and a contract with a cryogenic lab, supposedly reputable and unexpectedly affordable.

Jon's heart-filled desire for continued connection with Henry persisted despite his knowledge that he would never see the same bird back again. If Henry's DNA ever created life, the circumstances that formed her new personality would be unique. Henry's loud domineering character would express itself differently from her time with us, a household of enablers. But Jon needed the eternal link of love symbolized by Henry's muscle tissues in a deep freeze. Some people comprehended our link to a greater love with other symbols: a cross, a star of David, a statue of meditating Buddha. Whatever worked.

I understood a youngster's attachment to the everlasting because I remembered it from my youth. At the time, I felt my childhood would never end: climbing the plum and cherry trees to gobble the best fruit, wrestling with Curly, the family mongrel who cleaned my face with copious licks, chasing boys around the school playground, diving so deep in the nearby lake that I could feel the crawdads at the bottom, falling in love with a dreamboat for the first time at age sixteen.

Although I cannot go back to childhood's positive sense of the unending, perhaps nature will do that for me as I age, as she does with many older folks whose minds grow evermore simple. Maybe this will be her way of preparing me to partake in a child's sense of the eternal before my Kelvins make their big change.

If my current bodily energies give me joy and feelings of connection to the everlasting, who knows how great my Kelvins might feel when, one day, they take the big rollercoaster ride into a new arrangement? There could be more fun ahead.

Chapter 25
Zooming Ever Lower

I have fallen in love with Zoom and other electronic meetings. Most people I know use this medium for group gatherings now, although it is fairly new, popularized during Covid. We became explorers as we felt our way toward this new communal experience. I have come to admire our collective frontier gumption.

With more people using digital get-togethers, I am delighted to see us all dip to lower meeting standards. I am only interested in behavior that's on the bell curve of the norm. I don't include the weird sex fetish meeting bombers in this survey. As we increase the normal human quirks rarely seen in office meetings, we balance sterile technology with human warmth.

A couple of weeks ago, I saw a woman, Eileen (as her label read), fall asleep as a group of 30 listened to a digital art history lecture. Twenty-nine of us watched her mouth hang open as she slumbered. Luckily, she remained muted, so we did not hear her snore. Art history lectures have always provided cures for insomnia. Having spent a career as an art history professor, I have done my part to rid the world of sleep deprivation. When I taught in real rooms, someone next to the sleeper jabbed him (usually a man). But a private typed chat message to Eileen by her screen neighbor would not wake her. If I unmuted and shouted her name, I would interrupt the venerable lecturer. In a physical meeting, I would not openly gawk at the sleeper, but online, I stared to my heart's content. I watched her, then I gazed at the slides of sublime Chinese Shang Dynasty bronzes from 5000 BC, then I observed Eileen again, back and forth like a tennis match.

The same week, I attended a digital group of 250, a worldwide meeting. The hosting group started the meeting in Seattle, but I joined from Hawaii, as did folks from India, Japan, Canada, and Germany. This group had met weekly for over six months, not a big deal anymore to them, though its international scope still astounded me. But I had not expected a bigger excitement. All at once, an American woman named Joan picked up a corn cob and proceeded to chomp on it throughout the meeting. Thrilled, I couldn't believe my eyes. A large ear of corn spread across her face like a huge, yellow grin which probably matched my big smile. Would she eat it typewriter style, left to right and back again? Yes, she did, just like I would. Did she know 249 people from around the world watched a close-up of her corn performance? I doubted it. She showed no awareness of being on view.

Real Life—Real Laughs

Did Zoom lull us into thinking no one could see us? I heard from a friend of a friend about a woman who forgot people were watching and used the bathroom during an online meeting. Luckily, she met with a small group of friends who kindly reminded her, "Jane, you do know that we can see you in the bathroom, right?" Apparently, Jane had forgotten people could see her. She used her smart phone and, I suppose, habitually carried it into the bathroom.

I have carried the same habits I used in real meetings into the computerized format. I always sit still, look up at the speaker, down at my notes, cross and uncross my legs, and sip tea occasionally. In every electronic meeting, I am astounded to see a person who constantly moves, so much so that it looks like a dance. In one such meeting, a woman must have waved a small device like a smart phone because her body seemed to flail sideways, then upside down, then right-side-up again, with arms and legs in non-stop motion. I could imagine her doing this for a minute or two while getting her phone properly set up. But after an hour, it seemed pathological. The human eye gravitates toward motion and I could not help watching the agitated form until I got seasick.

In almost every online meeting, at least one person keeps their face dark, in shadow, sometimes all features obscured, a black hole. In one small weekly Skype group, a friend always had a blank visage. I found it odd to speak to a dark space on top of shoulders. I didn't want to call her Darth Vader, but I did, just once. I subtly asked if she could put more light on her beautiful face. I would rather talk to her than to Darth Vader. She acquiesced, but the next week, she had gone back to the dark side again. I let her be.

In warm Hawaii, people routinely wear little clothing. But it still shocks me when an online meeting participant's male family member walks through the Zoom background shirtless, especially a son or grandson, young and hunky. My girlfriend's teen-age daughter routinely wears short shorts and a sports bra as she wanders around behind her mom on Google Meet. While considered perfectly appropriate wear for a teen-age girl in Hawaii, somehow it shocks me every time she suddenly flashes onscreen. My eyes focus on the bare skin, and I forget the topic at hand.

A distant friend, Derrick, used his bed as his Zoom background. Sometimes his bed remained tousled from the night, sometimes not. I never considered myself a fussy soul, but I feel unable to reveal the personal terrain of my bed to the world. After a month or two of meetings, I asked if this was, indeed, his real bed. Somehow, if it had been a guest bed, I would have felt better. He seemed proud and said, "Yeah. And I have a big screen TV so I can lie here and watch Netflix." At that moment, I

Real Life—Real Laughs

realized, unconsciously, I had put him on a pedestal for being president of a prestigious private school and for his excellent work with charities. Staring at his bed each week and imagining him sprawled while watching movies humanized him. I took him off the pedestal.

It amazes me to see how many people on Zoom reveal half their face, usually the top section, the forehead, eyebrows, and half-closed eyes; not the most flattering features. People seem to lower their eyes to type or stare at their screens located below their neck, perhaps laptops in their laps, making their chin, mouth, and sometimes their nose disappear. Today, for the first time, Jason showed half his face, vertically. I saw one eye, half a nose and half a mouth for the whole meeting. I wanted to ask Jason if he did this on purpose, displaying his best side. But at this business meeting, I demurred, trying to keep a professional demeanor.

One woman, leading a meeting, apparently needed to peer closely at the screen. For the whole hour, we saw only a huge eyeball, not the most flattering look.

Because of Zoom, I have never seen the tops of so many people's heads as they apparently lower them to read or write something. I now know that my family doctor has very few hairs up there. At our tele-health computer meetings, I have counted them; there used to be 48. Now there are 36. I have not mentioned this to him.

People who use their smartphones or tablets seem to favor the giant hand gesture. In the middle of one meeting, all at once, a huge organic shape swooped in, as if attempting to grab a viewer at close range. Once I got over the shock of a wrinkled behemoth seemingly launched towards me, I realized the person had their device situated such that it showed their hand moving forward to change a setting. I would think the person would notice how ugly and disturbing this move appeared.

I have not mentioned people's animals and children galumphing through our meetings. Those cute and sometimes loud beings have become commonplace in digital workspaces. In office assemblies of old, we did not see someone's bed. No one munched an ear of corn. Half-naked relatives didn't prance around the focused group. We saw our cohorts' full faces, all exposed to the same lighting. Animals and children were strictly verboten.

Because individuals set up their electronic meetings at home, each participant almost can't help but project a sense of cozy privacy while trying to maintain business-like formality. This contrast creates a jolly anomaly. I adore this creative fusion of private and corporate, when the messy human bits intrude into pristine, elevated business customs. In almost every cyber-meeting, with admiration and a laugh, I find new joy in my fellow meeting mates. If this trend remains strong, it seems likely online meetings could evolve to make business culture more humane.

Chapter 26
Red Bed

Kaethe Kauffman, **Kaethe Kauffman's Bed**, *photo, 2021*

During Covid, I dyed everything on my bed red. This desire came over me in a rush. All at once, I dumped bright dye in the washing machine, followed by sheets, pillowcases, a bedspread, shirts, nightgowns, pajamas, and underwear. My eyes danced with the visual feast that emerged. Every night I wallowed in varieties of scarlet. Each fabric took the dye differently, so I enjoyed hues from salmon orange to hot pink to Christmas red to soft rose.

I had loved my formerly white sheets, 700 count Egyptian cotton. I had them monogrammed with my original name which I had reclaimed after a bad breakup, a symbol of my new life. The sheets featured thousands of tiny bumps, and I loved the soft texture. As years went by, I patched several small holes. One day, when I tried to brighten the white sheets by washing them with Clorox, the bleach caused large beige/ochre stains which bore an unfortunate resemblance to urine. Nothing removed those stains. The rebel in me said, *No, I refuse to throw away these noble sheets.* This led me to grab the old dye bottle, which happened to be nearby.

My wild red spree didn't seem inspired by frustration with the pandemic. Ten years ago, I did the same thing with purple dye, tossing in shirts, pants, and small clothes. I spared my bed on that round. But I felt resplendent in the new shades I donned, from lavender to deep royal hues. Friends noticed and were kindly inquisitive about my new clothes. But these colors didn't bleed in subsequent washings with other fabrics, unlike red.

I had "fixed" the red colors in a special substance designed to stop any bleeding into other fabrics. But eventually all my towels, washcloths, kitchen linens, and more underwear turned pink. The red dye spiraled out of control. Everything in my home now matched. I would not change a thing. I preserved my favorite sheets, luxuriated in warm colors each night and cheered up my home with rosy accessories.

I began to think of other impulsive decisions I had made in the past: who to date, where to travel. The consequences of some of these had, like red dye, bled into the rest of my life for years, sometimes turning it more cheerful like the pervasive pinkness in my home. People I met in Czechoslovakia in 1967 became my friends for life. Now, our children keep in touch.

At other times, the consequences could be more dismal. A couple of bad breakups come to mind. I would not have changed all the good inherent in these relationships at the beginning and the valuable lessons I learned about how to communicate better with people. However, I still grieved the deep sadness of our final partings, a permanent stain on my life.

Several years ago, a significant major unplanned event arrived: Covid 19. Like red dye, it spread. Throughout the huge changes in our routines, I remained resolute, making the best of it, as have most of my friends. But one colleague showed up on Zoom meetings and, each time, angrily ranted about how she hated having her usual routines upset by the pandemic. I haven't yet mentioned to her that this terrible disease has probably been more inconvenient for those who have died. It has been tempting.

On the other hand, she made me realize that like my red bed that has continued to spread cheerful pinkness throughout my home with each load of laundry, my initial pandemic decision to roll with the punches has given me a more positive attitude in the long run. On lockdown number one, I discovered how to order food from grocery stores, and have it delivered. I now love keeping in touch via electronic meetings, which would not have happened so pervasively without this national emergency. Over the unexpected year plus of solitude, I enjoyed socially sanctioned introversion: reading, writing, painting, drawing, meditating, and journaling. Just as my red bed spawned cheer in my home, a mostly positive attitude toward the pandemic has led me to new joyful discoveries.

Chapter 27
In the Dark

I spent thirty years in dimly lit rooms with strangers, so I am an expert on what people do in the dark. As an Art History professor, I greeted students, fired up the projector, and turned off the lights. Then I commenced enlightening them with the most thrilling visual insights humans have experienced throughout history, from the sophisticated and eerie perspective in pre-historic cave paintings to the agonizing existential scream of Edvard Munch.

Many students instantly fell asleep. Once, a snoozing guy fell off his chair. The ones who stayed awake picked their noses; it's amazing how many people did this when they thought no one would notice. The alert students also sneaked looks at their cell phones below desk level, strictly verboten.

Students' sleeping sickness remained a mystery to me. I made jokes, widely gestured, and raised my voice to impart passion. My enthusiasm proved contagious to many students, but a minority seemed to have an on-off switch in their brain: dark equaled sleep.

While bequeathing secrets of the sublime to my

Real Life—Real Laughs

students, I also took on policing duties. I abandoned the podium to wander the aisles with a remote clicker changing the images. When I saw a nodding head or a suspicious glowing lap, I walked to that person and stood near as I continued my talk, raising my volume, thus causing other students to titter, to glance at me and the errant student. I wasn't above public shaming. It worked.

Once I started this vigilant program, I rarely had another sleeper or cell phone sneak. Nosepickers persisted, but I went easy on them because their eyes stayed on the screen.

One summer, I took vacation time to attend a meditation retreat. I needed downtime to rest. Anyone who has meditated knows that, as part of the process, random insights pop into mind, whether you want them to or not. I thought about my career and realized that I functioned as a guide for my students. But who guided me? At times I have sat in the dark and could have used someone to comfort me, to remind me to listen, absorb the good, and do the right thing.

In reality, when trauma struck, I envied the students who fell asleep. I preferred to obliterate chaos by ignoring it. During my meditation retreat, I couldn't help thinking about two nasty events that completely threw me. They had hit at different times, several years apart. But when one struck, I felt blinded, thrust into a black unknown. And, each time, I would have chosen deep unconsciousness.

One terrible day, when I was 51 years old, Mom suddenly died from a blood clot in her brain. Normally unflappable, on that day, I flapped like a trapped bird in a cage. I envied my students who could blot out reality with sleep. I would have welcomed a blackout but remained sadly insomniac. Several weeks later, when my tears would not stop, I needed spiritual help to climb out of the black hole.

I did not belong to a church, but I had been attracted to a Buddhist temple I had once visited. In desperation for solace and answers, I called and asked if the woman minister would see me even though she didn't know me. Reverend Nan said, "Come now." She became a soothing helpmate at a critical time. I joined the temple to help me maintain useful practices.

Five years after Mom passed away, I needed to separate from a long-term partner. A week before I moved out, I anxiously planned and packed. During that week, my heart felt like it was beating in my throat as I moved around in a dark, panicky cloud. I felt too rushed to get eight hours of sleep, let alone sink into a mindless void all day and night, which I would have welcomed.

Real Life—Real Laughs

In the middle of one night, I awoke with so much pain in my chest, I assumed I had suffered a heart attack. After a few hours, the pains subsided. I didn't want to bother anyone, so I waited until the next day when my friend Jane dropped by. When I mentioned my ghastly night, she recognized a panic attack and insisted I go to a doctor. As I went through the medical processes involved, Jane held my hand, always available and reassuring.

My thoughtful helpers came and went according to their expertise and my needs. I have rarely seen Nan or Jane in the past few years. But when I think of them, warmth bubbles up within me for their steadiness and sympathy that, at the right moment, illuminated my obscurity.

No matter what future emergencies might occur, I have learned that the option of zoning out to escape a bad experience doesn't bring true comfort. I have developed a bedrock faith that compassionate souls emerge at the right time. Palpable good exists, like a force-field or an entity, available when darkness falls. Like a slide show of great art in a dim room, from the Sistine Chapel in Rome to the contemporary Mark Rothko meditation room in Houston, helpers lighten the dark, making it sacred.

Chapter 28

Crazy

The other day, while walking out my front door, I found myself glancing down to make sure my shirt was buttoned. Then I laughed. I had caught myself doing one of Mom's Sanity Checks. She always told me, "If you forget to button your blouse, that's a sure sign you're looney."

My mother passed away, but her self-checks about how to assess my saneness have stuck with me. Now I wonder why she felt so concerned about our basic lucidity. As a child, I don't remember hearing anything on this topic from the other neighborhood moms.

Lipstick going too far away from the lip line signaled mental instability. Bra straps and slips showing more than a few inches for prolonged time periods, an absolute taboo in the 1950s and early 1960s, meant a person might go crazy at any moment. Mom convinced everyone that the neighbor's foster son was a typical sociopath and described this abnormality in detail to me for decades. At the time, I assumed she knew the correct facts. In reality, I don't remember the handsome teen-aged boy doing anything askance.

Real Life—Real Laughs

Mom attributed female psychological problems to pioneer history. My grandparents had been homesteaders in the 1800s, building a log cabin in the tall timbers of the Pacific Northwest rain forest. According to Mom, women stuck in these tiny, dark hovels, with their husbands out working all day, gave rise to "cabin fever," or what she called, in the 1950s and 1960s, a "nervous breakdown." Blouses buttoned wrong or slips showing could escalate into full-blown homicidal or suicidal catastrophes. That is why she emphasized checking our buttons, bras and slips—to stop a cognitive blip before it got out of hand.

At age 12, I remember my backwoods' homesteading grandmother, 89 years old, deciding to take a nap after Thanksgiving dinner. She quietly passed away with a turkey-filled stomach. Grandma, a music teacher, always impressed me as accomplished and intelligent, supremely sane. I never heard stories about her going berserk in a log cabin.

I don't know where Mom's concern about madness came from. However, she loved to create high drama, and absurdity always got people's attention.

Mom projected the image of an exemplary woman, college-educated and smart. She loved brinksmanship, pushing herself to the edge as a self-styled liberated individual who had mastered the latest knowledge in her field, who also partied with enthusiasm. As a Special Education teacher, she quietly used hypnotism to help her students relax and learn more efficiently. In the days before mainstreaming, her classroom was separate from the main body of the school and she designed her own curriculum.

After school, she immediately repaired to the local watering place and enjoyed the first of her evening vodkas, insisting that her habits constituted the superior way to live. As she aged, the 5pm vodkas began to start as early as 3pm. I found it impossible to communicate with her at these times, for she behaved like a typical drunk: narcissistic, cruel, and nonsensical. I considered her insane when inebriated. But she never checked her blouse buttons at those times, for she didn't appear to doubt her brain function when soaked with vodka. She seemed to feel entitled and criticized me for not drinking and "having fun" with her.

When I reflect on it now, I find supreme irony in her unrecognized mental obliteration each afternoon and evening. I suppose part of the definition of mental illness is non-awareness of dysfunction. Looking at myself, as far as I can tell, I am not any nuttier than I've ever been. However, I might just be unaware. For this reason, the older I get, I'm continuing to use Mom's Sanity Checks.

Part Four
Being Brave or Not

James Haydn Kauffman Hite, **Kaethe Kauffman Jumping, Halona Beach Cove, Oahu, Hawaii,** photo, 2014

Chapter 29
Cliff Jumping

Standing at a cliff's edge, I gauge the expanding swell of a wave as it pushes its apex up the rock wall. If I catch the surf at its highest, I jump about thirteen feet. If I miss it, I plunge twenty-five feet or more. All at once, I'm ready. When the water upsurges to its maximum, I push myself off the edge, hold my nose and drop.

For most of my childhood, I grew up immersed in the neighborhood lake, playing water games, diving from docks and boulders, swimming for hours. As I hit the water now, the ocean's cold embrace brings back my ecstatic feelings of youthful exhilaration. Luckily, I have leapt far enough that I'm not shoved back against the rocks, which would have left a scraped hulk for my adult son, Jon, to rescue.

I shared a fun day at Jon's favorite cove on Oahu, picturesque with high cliffs around turquoise waters that transform into pounding surf surging against the rock walls and up to the small beach. It is so gorgeous; *Pirates of the Caribbean* used it as a film set. The real reason I hurl myself into space and plunge into the ocean at age 68 is that I want to prove I'm not an old fogey, and I can still share outdoor adventures with my son.

Compelled by the same impetus, several weeks later, we went parasailing, an experience that mimics the process of death. As the giant sail pulled me off the boat, I faced possible imminent disaster and sprang into the unknown. Having worked with hospice patients for six years, I have seen these folks display enormous courage as they take a similar leap into the vast mystery.

Strapped into what felt like a flimsy harness—multiple straps around our thighs, rear end, and waist with vertical ropes attaching us to the sail above—I felt the wind tug me toward the back of the boat, the launch pad. My foot scraped along the boat's surface as long as it could, then reluctantly lifted as I was pulled aloft by the inflated rectangular parasail swooping behind the speeding motorboat. I had no choice but to completely let go, to submit to nature's forces swirling around me.

Could this possibly be worth the terror? As I flew into the air, I clutched the vertical ropes that held me, my knuckles literally white. My son and I, in paired harnesses, swayed in the gusty breezes. I was happy he soared near me, about twenty feet away.

We hollered back and forth. "Are you okay?" he asked.

I gave him the thumbs up sign which, for me, meant, *I'm terrified but still alive.*

"Are you scared?" I shouted back at him. In response, Jon let go of his hold on the vertical ropes and leaned back, holding his arms out wide, as if embracing the sky. A lightning bolt of fear zipped from my groin up to my throat. My mind could see he was perfectly safe, well-balanced in the harness. But my fingers grasped all the harder on my slender straps. If I kept looking at him, I would vomit.

I forced my head to look elsewhere. I was struck by the silence and the blue world. The horizon disappeared as ocean and sky blended into pure azure beauty, a divine space where I hung suspended, a part of the whole. I hoped this was what death was like because it was more than worth the panic. It was proof that terror can transform into elation.

My cliff leap and parasailing make me ponder the other reasons I have flung myself over several of life's precipices. Aside from proving my female machisma, other extreme experiences are societal rites of passage that our culture elevates, although they require taking permanent, sometimes life-threatening risks: marriage, pregnancy, childbirth, and child-rearing.

I give my utmost to each challenge. I am never perfect. But I ended up with some integrity when I terminated a 25-year partnership, both a business and romantic relationship. Despite that upheaval, I was able to keep a marvelous closeness with my son, Jon. I survive each thrust into the unknown with a ragged self-respect, like a tail, still wagging behind me.

Another plummet into the great beyond with lasting consequences was surgery. I'll admit to having a doctor put me under general anesthesia to strip an enormous varicose vein out of my leg. It resembled a knotted and twisted ship's rope under my skin. I succumb to collective beauty standards for legs.

A few years later, an appendectomy and a lumpectomy for breast cancer saved my life. I face each experience as best I can. Several months later, I feel profound gratitude for modern medicine and a supportive culture that allows me, an ordinary citizen, to receive the best medical care imaginable.

I notice that surgery resembles cliff-jumping. Once I find myself on the table, the anesthesiologist ready to push the plunger, I'm committed, come what may. I say prayers and place ultimate trust in the mysterious medical process that consumes me, just as I did with cliff leaps, parasailing, relationships, childbirth, and child-rearing.

Apparently, I am willing to take the big risks for several reasons: to bond with Jon, to fulfill life's rituals, and to keep my health.

I imagine one day I'll accept that my old bones aren't up to leaps and flights. In the future, I might be able to let go of health, to accept when it's time to tumble off life's edge into a Buddhist Pure Land. I hope my practice at cliff jumping prepares me for the final leap.

Chapter 30

Paint Boxer

A wiry older woman, Glenna, marched alone into an abandoned arena. Built in the same year Glenna was born, 1948, she hoped she didn't look as decrepit as the peeling paint and exposed rebar around her. The 20,000-seater showed its age, even though the building had enjoyed its last game only a few months earlier. At the thought, she automatically patted down her natural curls, a vain gesture, for her shoulder-length silver hair sprang from her head, seemingly as excited as she felt.

Glenna had taught drawing and painting for many years to children and adults. Now retired, she painted and drew for her own pleasure. Locking the door from inside, she exhaled a quick breath. Sweet solitude.

In this spot, sports teams and musicians had played to cheering thousands. Last week, a close friend from City Hall tossed her a key and invited her to use the stadium, due for demolition in a few months. "Do anything you want there," her buddy said with a wink, as if she expected the bizarre.

"Happy to oblige," Glenna said. She caught the key in mid-air and ran out the door, calling, "Thanks," over her shoulder.

Beige walls stood bare, the seats removed. When Glenna flicked a switch, her hair gleamed like a rock star's, lit by hundreds of overhead lights shining in the vast space. She explored, for she loved old buildings. The plain walls reminded her of a humongous art studio, brimming with potential. When she spotted a crate of old boxing gloves in the corner, her eyes widened, and she made a mental note to return. Meandering, she found left-over oversized paint cans: red, blue, yellow, orange, purple, green. *Well, why not?* she thought, waltzing back to the boxing gloves.

In the 1950s, when boxing enjoyed a reputation as the paramount self-defense, her father gave her lessons. Looking upward, she sent a prayer to her dad who had wanted the best for her. "And look what I have now, Dad," she said to the air above as she waved her arms toward the dilapidated structure as if it were a palace. "It's great, isn't it?"

When she donned the gloves, they swiveled on her small wrists. She pulled the ties tight and took a few swings for old times' sake. Her muscles remembered and wanted more. She felt a surge of vitality knowing she could still be a tough girl. After trotting to the line of paint cans she had opened, she surveyed the bright colors while she pumped her arms in boxing moves. Inspired by her agility and the array of hues, without thinking, she quickly dipped a glove in yellow. Prancing around, she lifted the soaked leather glove and took a swing at the wall, as if she were still in the old backyard ring. Under her fist, a satisfying splatter of paint exploded like a bursting sunflower. She loudly laughed.

Next, her yellow glove plunged into black paint; she didn't care if the colors merged. In black, with bits of yellow, she drew a long curve that wound around the wall in a wandering line. As she bent, then stood on tiptoe to get the line just right, she could have been dancing a post-Martha Graham frolic. Now she bathed two gloves at once in purple and green and plopped great rounds of color in giant polka-dots. Feeling like a child, she giggled with glee. The paint looked delicious, and she wanted to slurp it off the wall like a warming ice cream cone. "Yum," she murmured as if tasting a peppermint flavor.

With colorful smudges in her hair, she glanced down at the black, yellow, purple, and green boxing gloves, now looking like two bruised eyes. When she twisted and turned them in tandem, they seemed to make fanciful facial expressions: fierce when drawn together, innocent when looking up, confused and cock-eyed when pointed inward, stunned when staring straight ahead. These eyes reminded her of how she had felt years ago when a drunken ex-boyfriend slugged her in the eye for no apparent reason.

At that time, 45 years ago, she escaped from the house and never went back, but apparently a residue of anger remained. She pretended to aim at him as she slammed a wet black glove into a blank wall. Savoring the impact of squishy paint, she ground her glove into the plaster surface. Next, she smeared dark blue to add a layer over the black. The mess resembled her old, damaged eye. When her wounded right eye had looked upon itself the second day, some green had appeared, so she sloshed jade highlights on the stadium wall, crafting a creative replacement for a bad memory. At this moment, feeling powerful, her actions were a perfect antidote to the old trauma.

With a deep breath, her chest expanded, and it seemed as if she could see the totality of the arena's huge space all at once, her dominion to command. Like a giant bird of prey, perhaps one of the elegant condors she spied in the Grand Canyon riding the thermals round and round, she could soar in her imagination, looking for the perfect spots to paint her visions. She eventually discovered a tall expanse near the main entrance that provided ample space.

Exhilarated, she craved round shapes, her arms ready to swing and swoop with their full range of motion, like the astounding circling condors. Intuitively, she allowed her arms to move as they wanted.

She knew round forms often symbolized spiritual unity. Like a schizophrenic who, given pen and paper, spontaneously drew calming disks for hours, she succumbed to the primal impulse and comfort of moving in circular flow. Her breath followed the circles in rhythmic repetitions.

Plopping her gloves in red and orange, she splashed paint in giant rings, as big as she could reach. Next, she added concentric shapes in pink, turquoise and yellow. If a small space appeared in the center, she aimed brown and black punches inside it. Paint flew. The splendid colors sagged and ran, merging into sloppy and surprising abstract miniatures within the larger design. Later, when she took close-up photos, these would be rich stand-alone compositions. Many spheres followed with more bull's eyes to fill. When her muscles demanded rest, she gazed upon thirty or more coiling shapes, a visual feast. As she enjoyed them, she breathed with her diaphragm in deep, slow rhythms.

Glenna knew she must look like a well-used drop cloth. But, after ten more multi-colored, layered swirls, taller and wider than her body, she felt satisfied. As she looked again at the many bright orbs, she chuckled for, all at once, she saw her murals as a carnival of dancing, vibrant breasts, bobbing around her. Although the impulse to paint circles had come upon her in a rush, unplanned, her subconscious apparently perceived an opportunity to celebrate happy breasts. Society foisted odd expectations on female anatomy: that it serve a decorative purpose to satisfy male expectations. Many women felt conflicts about their chests, so Glenna thoroughly enjoyed celebrating this essential part of women's bodies.

Smiling, she threw one more punch spawning bright red splashes. What good work on the first night. With a deep gulp from a water bottle, she surveyed the festive walls, festooned with vibrant colors and shapes. She breathed in their glory.

With three more months until demolition, she would explore the infinite designs whirling in her mind, her hands eager. Plus, she had planned to use five decades of sketchbooks with scenes and abstractions ready to fling into the waiting spaces. With enough boxing gloves, she would fill the stadium walls, and host a big party the night before demolition.

Looking at her work, Glenna felt a kinship with the Hindu goddess of Creation and Destruction, Kali. Although opposite processes, each one fed the other and continued in an endless cycle. Glenna would bless the old stadium with her paintings, photographing and videotaping all of them. She might exhibit the photos and videos if they proved to be good enough. In the future, she could print any size she wanted on canvas, paper, wood, or aluminum and continue to paint or draw more into it, transforming the design. Maybe she had finished with the themes of black and blue eyes and joyful breasts. But, if not, she would bring them back in new incarnations.

Chapter 31
Age Glorious and Victorious

Kaethe Kauffman, **Self-Portrait Rainbow**, *pencil, oil, 14"x11", 2022*

Deep within my mental recesses, aging's ever-lowering beauty standards joined with an odd gratitude for having survived this long. In my seventh decade, various faltering body parts, while not severe, nevertheless reminded me to appreciate that most of my appendages functioned at full tilt. Historically, our generation lived longer than any in the past. I wanted to celebrate this miracle.

Signs of my progress toward old age abounded. Previously, I had not realized how lovely it was to have skin firmly attached to my muscles and bones, as it had been until I reached my fifties. When I first noticed a hunk of my thigh drooping, outlined by long lines in my skin, as if sections were basted together with sewing thread, I thought I had developed a dread disease and rushed to telephone the doctor. When dialing, I realized, instead of a cascading skin sickness, this might simply be aging. I hung up, stunned that this had happened to me and that it was so ugly.

One day, my friendly Japanese American massage therapist touted a Japanese village he visited where he said people didn't age. "The skin on their arms doesn't even wrinkle," he said as he began to rub almond oil into my right arm.

"I guess I'd better move to Japan," I murmured, knowing he had observed my loosening arm skin. And I had been proud I had not yet developed full-fledged upper arm flaps.

Real Life—Real Laughs

I have been luckier than others. Some friends have had crippling diseases and others have sadly passed away. During poignant moments when I mourned, I knew how fortunate I had been. I felt I should do more to celebrate the miraculous things I could still do. But I usually took these feats, like climbing stairs and walking, for granted.

Looking back to my college years, I had not appreciated my left eye until, one night, I lost my vision. Cramming 24 hours for freshman finals prompted a sudden night-blooming abscess that blocked the tear duct. By the next week, my left eye had dried out and sunk deep into my head cavity, blind. With one eye, all reality became two-dimensional; stairs or slight depressions in the earth were invisible. Like a drunk, I wobbled and fell. Because I couldn't see anyone who approached from the left, I spent 50 percent of my time startled and staggering backward. But no matter how foolishly I stumbled, I couldn't cry about it. Or rather, I could cry out of my right eye. But one-half of a cry hardly counted.

On the bright side, I spent my college freshman year looking like a pirate, a black patch tied to my head, delightfully distinctive.

Four surgeries later, the eye healed due to the radical and courageous efforts of Dr. Richards of the Seattle Eye Clinic, who I forever bless. Although the left side of the world looked like oatmeal for a while, the heroic optic nerve sorted things out and I no longer lurched as though inebriated. When I saw three-dimensional sparkling space again, I rejoiced and soaked it in so greedily, I craved to capture it on paper and canvas. During those difficult college years, a life-long career in art was born. Along with it, I gained permanent appreciation for rich ever-changing lights, shadows, and colors in the world around me.

Remembering my born-again eye and in the spirit of aging-positivity, I noticed, in my sixties, that my cheekbones became prominent. Good. For years, I emulated fashion magazines, applying a darker shade of make-up below my cheeks to highlight them. At last, nature did one good thing to my face over time. She made my cheekbones stick out with natural shadows underneath, whereas everything else on my face got baggy: eyelids, under the eyes, folds of skin beside my mouth, and along my jaw.

Imagine my surprise when I went for a beauty consultation at a spa and the aesthetician told me I should fill in the hollows under my "way too prominent cheekbones" with the latest artificial chemical filler.

"What?" I cried. "You want to destroy my elegant model look?"

"Well, actually," the aesthetician replied, pointing at my visage in the mirror, "those bones combined with the sunken areas beside and under each eye feature your head bones. That's your skull sticking out, more and more each year. Very unattractive."

Heat flushed from my soft jowls up my face. I was surprised that I felt embarrassed about my skull showing.

As an artist, I had spent years drawing and painting the shapes of heads and faces, finding their exquisite contours enthralling. Was my own skull now ugly? *Never*, I muttered to myself. Out loud, I said, "I'm fine with my head the way it is. There's no need to fill in anything."

Deep within myself, I started a private Skull Pride movement and began painting bald self-portraits eliminating my hair in my imagination. I wanted to witness the full glory of my skull. The pictures aren't pretty but filled with splashes of expressionistic paint in rainbow colors, energetic and emotive.

I had a blunt friend, Annie. When I asked her if I should start ignoring signs of aging, her answer was immediate, "I can't imagine you doing that. You cling to mistaken illusions of eternal youth and beauty." My blond, blue-eyed power-house friend had a wrinkled face of her own and gave me a stern look, the lines around her mouth and eyes becoming more pronounced.

Although tempted to turn the conversation to the weather, instead, I reluctantly confessed she was right. I finally understood the defined cheeks and the hollows around my eyes did not depict youth. Looking at my skull and gravity-pulled skin, I confronted the evidence of passing years. "But," I pointed out to Annie, "I choose to paint and love my ever-more-obvious skull. Surely, this is a sign of mature acceptance."

Annie arched her eyebrows, "We'll see." She knew me too well.

I could love my skull and accept unlovely aging while maintaining optimism. I would show Annie. But I didn't tell her about my regular facials and laser treatments to de-wrinkle my face. Acceptance only went so far.

I felt as though the gerontology gods challenged me to be positive: to celebrate with creativity and gratitude, if I took the dare. With Annie and the aesthetician keeping me honest, doctors maintaining my physical parts, and brandishing my paint brush, I felt up to the task.

Chapter 32
Halo Meditation with Clouds

Kaethe Kauffman, **Halo Meditation with Clouds***, acrylic, oil, collage, 22"x20", 2019*

I do not paint human figures with eyes gazing downward. It is too depressing. Traditionally, martyrs stuck with arrows look down in agony. Or virgins modestly cast their eyes at the floor, a servile ultra-feminine ideal.

Imagine my surprise when I paint a larger than life-sized meditating woman with a halo and weathered body, but upright and strong, who insists on looking down. "No," I say to her, "that's not allowed. Your eyes go up and confront the world like any self-respecting meditation warrior."

But when I read her facial features, she seems to retort, "I look down with pride and power. Deal with it." Her chin angles up in what might be a supplication to a heavenly deity.

That is how she fools me at first. When I paint her face thrust upward, as if to search the stars, I am lulled into complacency. But my tricky fingers draw her eyes cast down without my awareness. Later, to my horror, I realized that I had joined millennia of artists who painted the horrible downcast gaze. But she mesmerizes me. Her expression remains riveting despite the eyes that look down. Oddly, her gaze focuses on me, even from its lofty position. She seems defiant, daring me to confront her.

I raise my voice to her, "Tell me, what's the deal with you? Are you filled with pride, defiantly grander than the rest of the world? If so, that's gross." I want her to have integrity, even if it means I must explore confusing thoughts.

Arguing with a painting is an artist's prerogative. As she evolves, the main character in any creative work gains a unique identity. I want my new friend to achieve a full personality, to express herself. This process takes strange twists and turns that I don't always comprehend or agree with. But, as my meditating woman gains power, I can't deny her. She has her way, and I leave her as is.

For years, whenever I have looked at her, I have been uncomfortable and repeatedly ask her, "What the heck are you thinking? Why do you look at the world that way?" My testy dialogue with her continues to this day.

Her haughty face dares the viewer to confront her. Perhaps she feels superior to others, a repugnant thought to me as a great lover of equality. Sometimes, I am uneasy and look away. But when I am resolute enough to question her, I understand that she values her strength and will not surrender it. Without saying a word, she is an outspoken woman. I fall in love with her air of command, her positive self-regard.

When I painted her, she allowed me to surround her with puffy clouds, dark as if filled with nourishing rain. The billows seemed to part around her, letting her bright oil and acrylic glory shine through. In actuality, the "clouds" consist of my mammograms, breasts squished flat and rounded by the tight clamps on a tortuous imaging machine.

I painted **Halo Meditation with Clouds** years before I had breast cancer, before I imagined I could possibly suffer from a disease that did not exist in my genetic lineage. At the time, I had no idea why I painted her with one breast missing, a jagged scar there instead.

That's weird, I often think. But my lovely creation shows her enormous strength to the world, regardless of a missing body part. I allow her to be exactly who she needs to be. In return, unbeknownst to me, she has prepared me to be strong for my road ahead. I adore her, so I painted a whole series of life-sized, one-breasted meditating women. I named one **Cancer Meditation** long before I imagined having cancer.

Ten years later, when breast cancer attacked, my cancer journey progressed, step by step. Fate happily allowed me to keep both breasts with complete healing, compliments of surgery, radiation and chemotherapy.

Halo Meditation with Clouds reminds me of my good fortune and I am truly overjoyed. It might have been otherwise, were it not for well-trained doctors and technology such as nuclear medicine and DNA tests of tumor cells. I have had no special treatment, only standard procedures. Every day I say prayers of gratitude.

Real Life—Real Laughs

I often contemplate **Halo Meditation with Clouds** on a large wall in my den and I see strength in spite of her body's suffering. She looks down to the depths. Her lowered gaze might include the empty space on her chest. If so, cancer doesn't scare her. She is gutsy while connected to the divine through her halo and reminds me to be the same. While my personal halo might be askew, I do my imperfect best to follow her meditating example.

Some critics say paintings should cause discomfort and prompt us to explore. If so, **Halo Meditation with Clouds** meets this standard. She comes from my hands and feels like part of me, so she probably mirrors an inner anxiety. When I question her, I interrogate myself. But, while I admire our mutual strengths, she disturbs me with her laser-like vision, prompting me to continue my questions to both of us: *Who are you? Are you too proud and stubborn, as some of my ex-boyfriends would claim?*

I can almost hear her reply, *Of course not. It's our right to be proud.*

I tell her, *You shimmer in an exultant splendor that is difficult for humans to behold.*

No one says this about me, but I love the spiritual dynamism she radiates. I struggle to express it in words. Meanwhile, I am content to learn from **Halo Meditation with Clouds**, always pestering me with her mighty, mysterious, and challenging presence.

Chapter 33
A Dentist's Secret

Last Thursday, much to my surprise, I saw one of my body's nerves. I never dreamed such a thing could happen. I had studied and taught anatomy and enjoyed viewing exhibitions that showed full-sized cross-sections of human insides. Some displays isolated the nervous system, so I had been aware of nerves' appearances for many years. However, my own nerves seemed well buried in my flesh. It had not occurred to me that I might someday see one.

A week ago, inexplicably, I had very low energy for several days and assumed I was fighting off a cold. When I developed a sore jaw right below two sensitive molars my dentist had been monitoring each month, I called him. He told me to come right in. X-rays clearly showed one of the suspect molars had flared up with infection. The nerves had died and needed to be removed in a procedure called a root canal. When he announced this to me, I shivered with dread and felt tears well up behind my eyes. In the past, whenever I had heard the term "root canal," people shuddered as if this were the worst kind of dental torture.

Real Life—Real Laughs

I prided myself on good oral hygiene and never thought that I would have to endure the vile procedure. I had to face it. I knew that any infection in my head posed imminent danger to the brain. I prayed hard. As it turned out, the actual procedure proved to be completely pain-free. Fortunately, the infection was small and had not spread. The dentist worked a full hour on my tooth. About one-third of the way through, when I could close my mouth for a minute, I asked if he had gotten into the nerve area yet.

He affirmed, "Yes, and in fact, you might soon smell an unusual, though typical odor of nerves."

"Really?" I asked, amazed. Somehow, nerves seemed as though they should be pristine, if not sterile. If they had any smell, it would resemble the fresh rainforest scent of laundry detergent.

Moments later, he announced, "I have your nerve here. Want to see it?"

With my mouth full of instruments, I grunted something I hoped he knew was, "Yes." My eyes opened wide and beheld a half inch strand that looked like a glistening brown embroidery thread with a tiny white pearl at the end. The dentist said the brown color indicated that the poor nerve had died. Normally, it would be infused with red or blue blood cells. Its shiny exterior and the drop at the end were my warrior cells that had fought invading bacteria and died, turning white in the honorable cause, otherwise known by the ignoble name of pus.

"Would you like to smell it?" he asked. While the assistant rinsed and suctioned my mouth, I said "Ehhhhh…" which he correctly interpreted as my assent. He put the small former body part up to my nose. A subtle scent wafted my way, ripe fresh meat, barely past its "sell-by" date, not a bad odor. It should not have surprised me. After all, much of my physical body was "meat." I felt excited. Not only had I seen my nerve, but I had also smelled it, an adventure beyond imagination.

The dentist kept working. My molar had two nerve canals. I felt him cease work in my mouth for a moment and opened my eyes to see him holding the second nerve up to his nose. It seemed that he had a habit of sniffing dead body parts. He caught my glance and gave me an abashed look. "Yeah, I always take a whiff, just to make sure." I would have laughed out loud if I could have. I had discovered a kinky secret of dentists. However, when I thought about it, it made sense to double-check the diagnosis. Because the human sense of smell is primeval, the correct scent might indicate how bad the infections were and would reassure him, at a deep level, that the procedure had been correct. But the vision of my dignified dentist sniffing nerves as a regular habit made me giggle.

On an ordinary Thursday, I had beheld one of my body's wonders, a nerve. What a thrilling experience. I also felt immeasurable gratitude for modern dentistry that healed me from a serious tooth complication, pain-free. In previous centuries, the infection of a tooth could cause terrible suffering, possible permanent injury, or death. How fortunate I felt to enjoy a long life in the twenty-first century and, as an added perk, be able to see and smell my nerves.

Chapter 34
Birds of a Feather

Kaethe Kauffman, **Eagle & Raven**, ink, 11"x 8", 2024

Browsing in Native Alaskan trading posts and chatting with folks, I was surprised to learn that eagles and ravens were called "lovebirds" by the Tlingit Native Americans. Many carvings and paintings depicted them together, as in this photo of a moose antler totem pole: the eagle above with spread wings perched on top of the raven below.

"How could these two possibly be 'lovebirds' when I have watched them fight in the sky day after day?" I asked the Tlingit shop owners, friendly young people eager to share their culture.

While in Alaska, I strained my neck peering in every direction, mostly up, to watch steely-eyed eagles. They loved the tops of trees and telephone poles, and I happily listened to their chortling and whistling sounds for hours. One startled me in the middle of a river, perched on a snag, apparently eager for a fish. As I floated by on an inflated raft, I called out, "Hi, Buddy," with delighted surprise.

Eagles seem to be hoarders, constantly adding to their gigantic nests weighing up to one and one-half tons. Commonly thought to mate for life, a biologist told me that, actually, they return to the same humongous nest each year and mate with whoever is there. They are more committed to their house than to a partner. I know human couples like that.

I also saw a lot of ravens in Alaska, widely considered

Real Life—Real Laughs

to be pests. But I loved their bold personalities. They seemed to watch every move people made and flew close, mingling with humans, cawing at us and each other in a language I could imagine learning.

As I watched them in Alaska, eagles and ravens looked like natural enemies, engaging in airborne battles like World War II Spitfires and Messerschmitts. Often, I would see a group of ravens dive-bomb a single eagle in aerial acrobatics, probably protecting their eggs and young from the doubtless hungry eagle who watched the agitated raven horde with seemingly majestic indifference.

When I asked the Tlingit shop-owners about these warring "lovebirds," they laughed and explained.

The Tlingit have two main clans, the Eagle and the Raven. We are forbidden to marry within our own clan, who are considered to be close cousins. But an Eagle can marry a Raven and vice versa. That's why we call them 'love birds.' Yeah, they'll probably fight, but that's nature's way, for birds and humans both.

I soaked in profound Native American wisdom. I had always assumed a good relationship precluded arguments. But that approach hadn't worked for me so far. Like the lovebirds, maybe I should give squabbling a try.

Chapter 35
Hooked

Kaethe Kauffman **Marilyn and Beloved Horse,** *photo collage, 10"x7", photo, 2024*

I am fascinated and hooked by another person's mystery, neediness, charisma, talent, or minor fame. Looking back over the years, I notice that I have been unaware when someone snagged me. How can I develop

Real Life—Real Laughs

awareness before I recklessly plunge into a risky relationship or volatile situation?

As an example, falling in love comes to mind. I truly believe, like Martin Luther King Jr., that I value people based on their character, not their color, the car they drive, their wallets, or their job. Even so, a cute guy with an intriguing job can hoodwink my better judgment. In the past, I have swooned at good looks, charm, money, and gifts of flowers. When a guy turns any of those in my direction, my knees shake, heat flares across my cheeks, and my internal dialogue kicks in, *Who, me? He's actually noticing me?* I am a low-self-esteem cliché in the romance department.

With time and practice, as I have slowly transformed my track record, I've learned to be careful while establishing affectionate connections. I have become choosy, resulting in periods of date-lessness during which I'm learning to love my own company.

The trick is to admit, *Yeah, I'm drooling over that guy's job and his fame. And probably his backside.* After allowing adoration time, I then realize he has foibles like everyone else, quirks I may or may not want to spend time with. Pausing to remind myself is the key, to allow a spark of conscious awareness. The moment of waiting is so important I name it the Sanity Pause.

Real Life—Real Laughs

Although it was not a date, when I met the Beach Boys' Mike Love at a small social gathering, I stuttered the whole time. Because I see myself as a strong, articulate person, I became confused and mortified at this unusual behavior. It is time to face the inner disconnect. I have realized I am human and it's okay to be swayed by society's idols.

New age wisdom tells women to become the kind of person they wish to fall in love with. Then they won't pursue their pipe dream in others because they already embody strength. While I am unlikely to morph into a rock star, I work at gaining a bit of financial security and I sing in a choir. I keep fresh flowers on my desk. My tiny efforts require conscious determination to be kind to myself. I have built up little bits of ongoing self-compassion that slowly evolve into self-respect. Maybe I won't stutter if I see Mike Love again.

More importantly, when an unconscious urge or a blast of emotion wells up within, I try to see the dangling hook before it snags me, I fall in love, or stutter. These impulses are as addictive as sugar or caffeine. The Sanity Pause—stop and reflect—works every time. If I crave a doughnut and coffee, I tune in to my body. When I turn inward, I find respect for the tingly energy powerhouse that runs through my veins and muscles. I ask these inner vitalities what would best nourish them. Daily, I make a vow to respect my body's deeper nutrition needs. This process happens quickly, in under a minute.

My sacred energies usually prefer a carrot. When I tell people this, they often scoff, "No way. You really want the coffee and doughnut." I cannot convince them that when I present my body with a sincere choice, my visceral cellular truth loudly hollers, *Feed me that delicious orange carrot goodness. Keep the icky sticky stimulating stuff away from me.*

After years of tuning in to my bodily systems, I have gained a peaceful cellular life, free of yearnings for chocolate and lattes, a major miracle. If someone puts a piece of cake under my nose, I won't argue and I enjoy it. But my body has no desire to seek it out.

A few years ago, a big self-pity hook, the size that could harpoon a whale, appeared in my life: breast cancer. My emotions leapt on the Poor Me roller-coaster, full tilt. With cancer, you are allowed this self-indulgence.

Friends, family, and therapists pampered me as I grieved. While I appreciated their concern, it was tempting to become an eternally wounded sufferer. But eventually I stopped and envisioned what my mind, body, and spirit really wanted: strength, clarity, and peace.

During my daily Sanity Pauses, I tune in to the inner coursing energies, feeling their miraculous aliveness. Abundant gratitude swells for peoples' caring attitudes and the many doctors, nurses, and technicians who have helped me. This joy overwhelms the self-pity tendencies.

During the quiet moments, I ask my body what she wants. I promise to honor her needs. When she says a loud *No* to certain chemotherapy, I refuse that chemotherapy, even when the doctor threatens me with certain death. I discover an alternative that my inner chemistry likes, along with another doctor who supports me. I gain a small measure of tranquility, especially a year later when I receive the magic "cancer-free" declaration.

I have been hooked many times and probably don't have full immunity yet from future snags. A surprising new glitz or emotional seduction might lurk behind the next bush. But, if pierced once more, I know to take a Sanity Pause. I will inch the hook out from under my skin and examine the gritty enticement. And if I meet another famous person someday, perhaps I will put some self-confidence on display and successfully articulate, "Hi, I'm Cate. How are you?"

Chapter 36
Being Brave—Or Not

Katy Fialova, **Kaethe Kauffman with Skull, Kualoa Ranch, Oahu, Hawaii***, photo, 2023*

Real Life—Real Laughs

After the recent bout with cancer, friends told me how brave I was. Really? I went through the shock of discovering that I, a vegetarian and (I assumed) immune to cancer, indeed had the disease. During a several month period of disbelief, I convinced myself, when the surgeon eventually dug around inside me, she would find nothing because:

1. I never had the illness in the first place. Someone made a big mistake.
2. On the off chance there had been a tiny tumor there, it had dissolved because I wanted it to. I called this positive thinking.

Denial did not seem heroic, so I kept these fantasies to myself. Numbly, I did what the doctors said to do, despite my disbelief: have more tests and succumb to procedures such as piercing the tumor with a titanium wire, marking its exact location. Weirdly, the thin wire flopped around outside my skin. I consented to the surgery, still convinced it would be fruitless. Although they had shown me sonograms and x-rays where they said a small blob existed, it looked like mashed potatoes. If it had sported a frowning face glaring at me, I might have been convinced.

Because I excelled as Queen of Denial, I recovered from surgery in good humor and peacefully waited a month for the tissue analysis. After the surgeon told me

Real Life—Real Laughs

she had removed a 1.2-centimeter tumor, I began to believe the rascal had actually existed. I listened to the results with a positive mindset because I have Pollyanna superpowers. I acquiesced to daily radiation for five weeks and a small round of chemo.

I started to believe I had experienced a real cancer episode. But it was mostly over by then. Radiation did not hurt and seemed benign. I tried and failed to imagine the quiet machine doling out silent second-degree burns, as happened to a friend.

During this time, I forged deeper links to my religious beliefs, more meditation and prayer. I am not sure this made me braver, but I felt more relaxed and responsive to my new reality as denial slowly receded. Once I finally accepted cancer had occurred, it unfortunately aroused distressing thoughts of death. Closeness to my Higher Power required perseverance because I needed to be honest. It was very hard for me to admit my flaws and Ultimate Consciousness didn't put up with phonies.

With sincere efforts at prayer and meditation, acceptance slowly seeped in: I was a creature with vulnerable flesh, just the same as all beings. With this came blessed compassion, for myself and others, a bit at a time. My religion, Buddhism, did not promise a rosy afterlife; it focused on building a positive consciousness in this life, which might carry over to the next. When I asked my

Buddhist minister if reincarnation existed after death, he replied, "I don't know." But my spiritual path emphasized gratitude, and I felt this in spades for these medical treatments that, as I finally comprehended, saved my life. Each day, sunshine became brighter, more treasured.

    I thanked the inner fortitude that kept me on track during my cancer journey, even when I lingered in complete denial. My process of acceptance wound along a curving path, sometimes subterranean, but always active, leading me toward emotional healing and an eventual understanding of reality. For this journey I needed resilience. But bravery? I stumbled through the cancer procedures, one by one, and never felt brave.

Chapter 37
The Last Laugh

When I was young, my best friend Charlene lived a few doors down and I spent a lot of time at her house. Her dad, Shuzo Yamane, a round-headed jolly guy, kept the jokes flowing, and their home felt like a living sitcom. I much preferred their house to mine.

Like most religiously lapsed Americans, Charlene's family did not attend their local temple, but contacted priests as needed for big events. They included me in their large, extended family celebrations, so I attended Buddhist weddings and funerals every year or so. As a result, I considered Buddhism to be as normal a religious choice as Christianity.

Shuzo's mom, Miyoko, 89 years old, lived with the family. Not quite five feet tall, two silver streaks ran through her short, dark hair. When I stopped by each day to do homework with Charlene, she giggled with us, sharing stories about her life when she was young.

"Can you imagine?" she would ask. "I reigned supreme as the Charleston champion of the eighth grade. With my short, bobbed hair, my parents practically disowned me. But they smiled when I headed to our farm's fields each day to take care of Heiwa, the strong bull I raised since he was a tiny calf. He followed me around and loved to be scratched behind his ears. He even walked me to school. No one ever dared to bully me. Charlene, you know what the word Heiwa means."

"Of course," my friend said, who had heard these stories before. "Your pet bull was named Peace."

"Oh, it was a perfect name for him," Miyoko said, her eyes shining, remembering. "He even won first place in the state fair in 1916. I thought the buttons would burst off my parents' coats, they were so proud."

With the Charleston and Heiwa times far behind her, Miyoko was the only devoted religious person I knew. She arranged flowers in the traditional ikebana style for the altar of the Seattle Betsuin, the largest Buddhist temple in the area. I remember the fragrance of cedar, pine and cherry blossoms surrounding her. Maybe her intriguing scent lingered and sent me on the path to becoming a Buddhist practitioner.

Charlene and I were working on a school project at her house one day when the phone rang. Charlene answered, then fumbled the phone, a look of panic on her face. "What is it?" I asked, rushing to her.

"It's obaasan," Charlene cried. "She collapsed in the temple." Her fingers shook as she called her dad. An ambulance had taken Miyoko to a hospital.

We later learned that, while arranging flowers in the temple, Miyoko's hands had faltered, and the flowers dropped to the floor. Trembling, she tried to remain standing, but soon crumpled next to her fallen flowers.

Miyoko held on in the hospital for a few days. On the third day, her large family gathered around her bed, surrounded by flowers. I stayed home because this was an intimate family gathering. But I mentally sent visions of flowers and sunlight to Miyoko, just the way she had taught me several years earlier. She had said I could relax, calm my mind and choose positive feelings and images to send to other people in need.

I easily imagined the Yamane family in their usual arrangement at serious family gatherings in an order I suspect originally derived from Confucius. Shuzo and his brother, the two eldest males in the group, always took the lead. Each gently touched Miyoko's shoulder. Their two sisters, forever second in rank, held their mother's hands. The two oldest male grandchildren laid a hand on an ankle. The two female grandchildren arrayed themselves around her toes, touching them or somewhere on her feet.

Charlene told me later that, all at once, the room's door had flown open and in marched Dr. Teitelbaum, an overweight oncologist with curly, bushy hair springing in

Real Life—Real Laughs

all directions from his head. Surveying the solemn scene, he bowed in respect to Miyoko and her family.

"Mrs. Yamane, how are you? I am here to examine you. Can you hear me okay?"

Miyoko feebly nodded.

When at last Dr. Teitelbaum wrapped his stethoscope around his neck, ending the exam, he leaned close to Miyoko. Looking into her eyes, he said, "I'm very sorry, Mrs. Yamane, but your journey is almost done."

Family members leaned closer to hear his soft voice. The doctor raised his volume, still holding her gaze. "But you are strong. I know that about you. And you are brave," he said to tiny Miyoko, frail as a dry autumn leaf about to be blown by a gust of wind. I imagined he spoke of spiritual courage and strength.

He pulled himself upright, puffing his chest out and raising his arms as if holding two slashing swords. Stomping his feet, like a soldier marching off to war, he yelled, "See me, Mrs. Yamane. Be like me, a courageous Samurai warrior. You can handle anything. Be tough, fearless. Be a Samurai." His arms slashed the air.

At the sight of the gesticulating Jewish doctor acting like a medieval Japanese soldier, the family cracked up with laughter, including Miyoko. Mid-giggle, with a broad grin on her face, and being held by her family, she slipped

Real Life—Real Laughs

into a final coma. Her shared laughter with loved ones was probably the last thing she felt and heard. Oh, that we all could be so lucky.

Later, Shuzo and Charlene, normally jocular, smiled somberly when they reported Miyoko's last day. They told me how grateful they were to Dr. Teitelbaum for helping to give Miyoko courage and joy in her final moments.

Several months later, Shuzo learned that Dr. Teitelbaum's parents had lost all their extended family in the holocaust. Shuzo and his three other siblings had grown up in a World War II Japanese American internment camp in Idaho. Miyoko had raised her children in the prison and helplessly watched her humiliated husband destroy himself with alcohol. Confined to the concentration camp for the duration of the war, the family lost their Washington farm. Unable to work the acreage, debts built up and they lost the property.

Dr. Teitelbaum and Miyoko suffered severe state persecution causing family deaths. And yet, both kept their humanity and, amazingly, a sense of humor.

When Shuzo and Charlene spoke about Miyoko, I gave them hugs because I missed her too. Privately, I sent prayers to Miyoko, thanking her for showing us a joyful departure and teaching me, from early childhood, how to search for the positive in my mind and send it to others, a happy habit I still enjoy every day. Throughout my life, I have remained close to Charlene and her family. When I think of Miyoko, I still send her mental pictures of flowers and sunshine.

Chapter 38
Shaman Joy

Kaethe Kauffman, **Shaman Joy**, watercolor, 10"x8", 2024

Who could resist this jolly mask carved out of yellow cedar by Tlingit artist Roy Watkins? Not me. I love happy art and when I found this turquoise lady, we seemed to be a divine match.

In native art, each carving told a story. When I asked the young, eager Tlingit trading-post clerk for this mask's tale, he said, "I'll call Roy to make sure I get it right." With the artist nearby, Juneau, Alaska seemed more like a village than a town.

Roy described the turquoise woman this way:

She is a shaman, symbolized by one eye half-closed in a vision quest. It is a good vision because of her big smile. The two small faces in the corners of her mouth represent spirits that are visiting her from the other world. Placed on her mouth, the spirits give divine wisdom, speaking through her voice. She likes what they are saying. Her hair is cedar bark, pounded to make it soft. Cedar is waterproof, so her hair keeps her dry, protects her.

Later, I learned that the young shopkeeper had pounded the cedar with Roy. The tongue sticking out on one tiny face symbolized "welcome." But it is also seen in the Tlingit war dance signifying courage. The concept of a brave welcome worked for me. I fell in love with her.

My blue shaman reminded me to keep the divine presence close and allow the sacred to find expression through me. I enjoyed spending time with her and often wondered what she saw in her visions: good welfare for the Tlingit? I, too, wished the same for my nearest and dearest. She has become a precious companion, her joy infectious to all who see her.

Author Bio for Cate Burns

Real Life—Real Laughs: Humor When You Need It Most, Cate Burns' collection of 38 humorous vignettes, has its roots in her childhood "Daily Diary," a padded pink vinyl diary with a well-used lock and key. She has continued journaling life's joys and absurdities to the present. This rich material, combined with Burns' family tradition of humor, both dark and light, inspires her ongoing explorations. Burns illustrates many vignettes with her original paintings, drawings, and family photos. She honors (or defames) the lineage in her maternal family that dates to the Scottish poet Robert Burns.

Real Life—Real Laughs

The author lectures and teaches internationally at universities in Prague, The Czech Republic, New York City, Los Angeles and many other cities. She has received grants and awards such as the Elizabeth Morse Genius Foundation Award and the Wu & Elsie Ject-Key Memorial Award, National Association of Women Artists, New York City, The Twentieth Century Award for Achievement, and the International Woman of the Year Award from the International Biographical Centre, London. She has won first place awards in the London Book Festival, the Amsterdam Book Festival, and the Paris Book Festival, the national Lorrin Tarr Gill Writing Competition, and the Pacific Rim Book Festival.

Past published works include an opinion editorial in the *San Francisco Chronicle*, San Francisco, California; opinion/editorial columnist, OUR TURN, *Tahoe World* newspaper chain in Northern Nevada and Eastern California; and a book of humorous essays, *Libido Tsunami: Awash with the Droll in Life* (2016, Savant Books and Publications).

Burns divides her time between Nevada and Hawaii.

www.ingramcontent.com/pod-product-compliance
Lightning Source LLC
Chambersburg PA
CBHW070138080526
44586CB00015B/1743